WHAT People Like You ARE SAYING…

"As a mom myself....oh wait...no I'm not...I really enjoy Kathleen's style – it's lucid and fun and humorous. I can see her being really popular and addictive in a good way."

- Brad Hall, Writer and Television Producer

"Inspiring and poignant, such a talented writer!"

- Amy Schiffer, Social Worker

"We have a saying in Farsi that fine artists should dip their hands in gold. Kathleen is one of those people."

- Jasmine Shofet, Elementary School Teacher Aide

"I related. Before reading Scraps I felt alone but now I know that my daily struggles are just part of life."

- Michael Yanez, President of CE Channel Consulting

"...Like reading letters from a great girlfriend. Each chapter sounds familiar yet original."

- Lynn Palmer, Interior Designer

"I nearly fell out of my seat laughing when I read this. Hilarious. Laugh out loud."

- Janeen O'Brien, owner, Clear Talent Group

"I laughed so hard I spilled my martini!"

- Alisa Davies, former Marie Claire cover model

Scraps

Scraps

If Life's Bits and Pieces
are the Ultimate Fortune,

Shouldn't I be a Millionaire by Now?

by Kathleen Melton

SCRAPS

If Life's Bits and Pieces are the Ultimate Fortune, Shouldn't I be a Millionaire by Now?
by Kathleen Melton

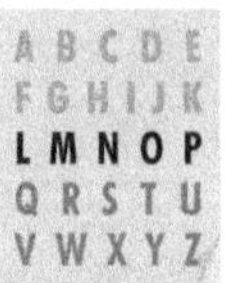

Visit our Web site at www.LMNOPublishing.com

Unattributed quotations are by Kathleen Melton.
All Photographs by Kathleen Melton or Keith Melton.
Cover Photograph of Kathleen Melton by Jessica Girard.

ISBN 978-0-9821140-7-0
Published by LMNOPublishing First Published 2009

Library of Congress Cataloging-in-Publication Data

Melton, Kathleen.
Scraps – if life's bits and pieces are the ultimate fortune, shouldn't I be a millionaire by now? / Kathleen Melton.
p. cm.

ISBN 978-0-9821140-7-0
1. Parenting & Family. 2. Humor. 3. Conduct of Life. 4. Happiness. 5. Los Angeles, California. 6. Entertainment. 7. Self-Improvement
I. Scraps. II. Melton, Kathleen.
III. Life's bits and pieces are the ultimate fortune.
IV. Shouldn't I be a millionaire by now?

Library of Congress Classification number 2008909289

Book Designed by Kathleen Melton and Leslie Sears.
Cover Design and book composition by Leslie Sears, LES is MORE Printing & Graphics.
Copyediting by Sheila Grimes.

Visit us on the web for more great books and products!
www.LMNOPublishing.com

MANUFACTURED IN THE U.S.A.

For Kendall and Kamden -

I gave birth to you and that is why I love you more.

Oh I'm lookin' for my missin' piece

Over land and over seas

So grease my knees and fleece my bees

I'm looking for my missin' piece.

Shel Silverstein, ***The Missing Piece***

A Note To The Reader

Like many of you, I live my life at the mercy of other peoples' schedules. Taxiing kids. Going it alone because of the all consuming business trips and endless meetings. Soccer practice. Baseball practice. Birthday parties. Work. Playdates. Ladies luncheons. The Nordstrom's Half-Yearly Sale. (Why is it only twice a year??) I am always in constant motion. Always dealing with time management issues. Always trying to keep up.

In that mix I struggle for my own identity. I work in and out of the home. I volunteer at school and in the community. I love my family. I parent our children. I embrace that which is other than mass-market idealism. I break from the political norm and (gasp!) vote my own moral conscience – not my spouse's, my friend's or even that of my political party.

Motherhood is wonderfully overwhelming and life is a constant moral, ethical and personal struggle to find where the true treasures lie. In my journey, I have discovered many gems and try to create a sustainable, peaceful and sane world for the future – our children. I also hope that one day, I may completely find myself.

Please take care of yourself during your journey.

With gratitude,
Kathleen Melton

Disclaimer

The purpose of this book is to entertain. The author and LMNOPublishing shall have neither liability nor responsibility to any person or entity with respect to any loss or damage caused, or alleged to have been caused, directly or indirectly by the information contained in this book.

Within the content of this book, trademark names may have been used. Rather than put a trademark symbol after every occurrence of the trademarked name, we used the names in an editorial fashion only, and to the benefit of the trademark owner, with no intention of infringement of the trademark.

The thoughts and views expressed herein are the sole views of the author and have been presented by the author and by LMNOPublishing for entertainment purposes only. The use of names of people and places known or unknown is purely for editorial content and meant to be beneficial to all parties in all ways known and unknown.

Contents

My Musings

From the Mouths of Babes

Contents

The Family That Plays Together....

Take A Stand

Contents

Safety Mom

Sexy Mama

Contents

Home Stretch

Excerpts from Kathleen Melton's column in the Los Angeles Daily News

My Musings

These are the scraps that fall right in front of your face.

That you step on and track through the house.

That continue to make a mess until you stop and pay attention to them.

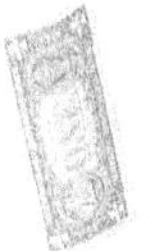

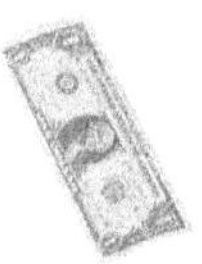

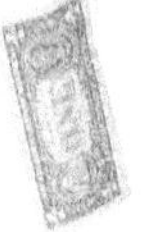

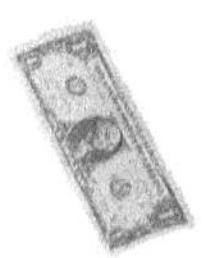

Not a Profession?

Standing and waiting for my stamp from the passport control officer in Casablanca, Morocco, I was suddenly jolted out of my exhausted state, "What is your profession?" He asked in French. "Pardon?" (My French ends at 'ou est la salle de bain?') "What is your profession?" He asked again, this time in English. This was an odd question as he had my declaration in front of him. "Mother." I said. He looked nothing short of harshly at me. "What is your profession?" he asked again. I suddenly felt afraid, traveling alone in a very foreign country where I did not even speak the language. And of the many hats I wear, Mother is my favorite job, and my most important. So, fear aside, I smiled at the passport control officer, and said, "Mom. I have children. I'm a Mom."

"That is not a profession." He said matter-of-factly, staring directly at me. Realizing I was in a country where women do cover themselves in shrouds, and that my fear should get the better of me, I still just could not let that pass. He was challenging me. "It's actually a round-the-clock job." I respectfully stated and smiled, hoping to get my point across and not be too insulting to this man who held the power of the 'stamp' that would allow me to continue my journey home! He "harrumphed" and laughed out loud, at me or with me? I couldn't tell. He gave me my stamp, still laughing, and excused me. I quickly moved on to my boarding area, vowing not to make another scene.

But I could not get the exchange out of my head. Motherhood not a profession? I could rattle off all the skills required and time put in to validate it as a profession, but truthfully, that won't affect the way this man viewed it. What would? I suppose if you look at it in the usual sense, we mothers do not receive monetary compensation. We don't get sick leave or health insurance. We do not have the luxury of two 10-minute breaks a day and an hour off for lunch. No minimum of a one-week vacation per year and no paid holidays. All this regardless of the fact that it is indeed a 24 hour a day 365 days a year job until the little tots leave home. And even then it's not like you can retire from this job. Whether you work outside the home in addition to being a mother, you are a mother first.

So what would validate motherhood as a profession to this man and so many others like him in countries around the world? As though stamping passports is somehow above raising children. What if he were to carry a child for 9-months? Go through the birthing process and then stay at home with that baby until they left for university?

This trip to Morocco was actually my first 7-day vacation off without my children in over six years. Among the women I know, the opportunity to escape on an adventure by oneself is the Holy Grail. We talk about it regularly. We fantasize about it. But rarely do any of us actually do it. Why? Because being a mom, our primary 'profession,' it's hard to find someone to 'fill in' for you while you are gone. Because no one but you knows the details and intricacies of your job. It's a bit harder to find someone to handle your kids' routines and schedules, your house, your spouse, the dog, and your work than it is to find someone else to rudely stamp a passport, but still, we moms should vow do it at least once a year.

So that's it. It is because we don't do it that we are unable to do it. Because we don't leave for 7 days at least once a year and have someone else step into our motherhood jobs. Because we don't take holidays or sick leave and have someone else fill in for us. Perhaps if we did take vacations and holidays and sick leave, perhaps if the men (and I realize some do) had to fill in and do our jobs for us while we were gone, perhaps then, around the world, there would be a greater understanding, that yes, motherhood is a profession.

Common Ground

What do you really want from your life? What do you think your elderly neighbor wants? What do you think the guy who packs your groceries wants? What do you think the young mother in Afghanistan wants? What do you think your child wants?

I think, I believe, that we all want the same thing – fulfillment, completion, being made whole. I go about finding my fulfillment, my completion, differently than you may, differently than a man may, differently than someone living in the Middle East may. We may all go about it differently, and we may all define it differently, but I believe we all want to feel whole, complete, and we want it to be lasting. Not fleeting.

So, play along with me here, if we all want the same things, why do we not celebrate our sameness? Our similarities? Why must we focus on the differences? On that which sets us apart? I can be an individual and still want the same things as you. I can have red hair, you can have sandy brown hair, I can be Christian, you can be Jewish, I can be a woman, you can be a child, but we can still want the same things.

I recently went to a musical event at a church (the acoustics were amazing!) that featured The Interfaith Connection. This musical group is made up of men and women from Jewish, Muslim, and Christian faiths that join their musical talents and voices in song to unite everyone in the room. It was magical at times. Songs that we all know, songs not 'owned' by any one religion or secular group, were sung in a round robin style in three or more languages at once. For a few moments, I actually felt the resonance of the world, of everyone in the room, young and old, from many different countries, from many different religions, all joined and cradled for that moment by the music, music that united everyone.

When it all comes down to it, we are all human. We all have a mom. We all want to live our lives to the fullest. And if we have children, we all want to see our children grow up, become adults and find their own fulfillment, their own happiness, and their own completion. Without the pain we may have known. Without having to bear any of the suffering that currently exists in our world today.

So I ask you to treat your neighbors, the seemingly rude woman at the market, the young out of control child, and the elderly gentleman in front of you, with the knowledge that they want what you want. That ultimately, regardless of language barriers, religious barriers, social barriers and yes, even, political barriers, we are all here for a reason. And we are all in search of that reason - trying to find it and fulfill it and complete it. And most of us are doing it the best way we know how.

Little Things

Six weeks ago I woke up with my head spinning. Literally. Violent vertigo. I fell over when I got out of bed. Got up and fell over again. My physician diagnosed a virus in my ear. Weeks later, various medications, a visit to an ENT, a Neurologist, an MRI and MRA of my brain (which were clear, thank God), the spinning continues. I was unable to drive for nearly a month. Unable to help my kids with their homework because the medicine blurred my vision. Unable to work. Unable to volunteer in my kids' classrooms. My husband picked up all the slack without complaint. I fell in love with him all over again. Then last Monday I had a "clear" day. I felt great in the morning. The spinning had subsided and I felt safe enough to drive. By one thirty in the afternoon I was so giddy with excitement that I was going to be able to pick my kids up from school that I was clapping my hands and singing around the house trying to make the time fly. Finally waiting outside my kindergartener's classroom, I felt like I had won the lottery. When his teacher opened the door and my son saw me standing there, his face lit up. "Mama! It's you!" he cried and ran into my arms. My second grader rounded the corner. His grin melted my heart. I stood there and held my two boys. To them, this was a sign that I was better, that our family life would go back to how it used to be. But I know that for me it will never be the same. I will never take for granted the privilege and the pleasure of being able to pick my kids up from school. It truly is the little things that have the biggest meaning in life.

My Spot

My kids have a special 'spot' at the dinner table and they will fight for it if someone dares to sit in it. They have a special 'spot' on the sofa and no one can breach it. Last Tuesday a woman at the gym became upset because someone else was standing in her 'spot' on the exercise floor. My friend and her husband invited us to their favorite 'spot' – a restaurant they frequent. Another friend escapes to a run down hotel up the coast – her get away 'spot'. And recently, I witnessed a man come into an office upset because someone had parked in his 'spot'.

All this got me thinking, where is my 'spot'? I don't really have a favorite restaurant. My 'spot' at the table gets taken over by the many frequent visitors and I squeeze onto the couch wherever I can. Sadly, I don't have a special getaway 'spot', and as for the gym, I can't imagine claiming any smelly carpet space as my own. Have I been living my life such that I am so used to having my needs bumped and putting others first that I know everyone's favorite spots but my own? I can think of past ones (before marriage and kids) but can't seem to think of anything specific for my life now. So I decide to spend some time thinking about and discovering my favorite spots. At this moment my 9 year-old walked into my office. He asked what I was writing about. I told him. He listened and with wisdom beyond his years replied, "Maybe you should focus on your spot in the world, Mama." I stared into the deep pools of his blue eyes. He always searches for the biggest – and in his mind the most obvious – answer. I hugged him and held him tightly. "This is a good spot," I whispered. "With us," he said. And as I tucked him and his brother into bed that night, I realized I've had a favorite and important spot all along, here as a mother to my boys.

Still...a beach spot would be nice....

Who Let The Dogs In?

Who invited dogs into my sanctuary? The place I go to escape, to zone out. The Mall. Now granted with two small kids a husband and a busy schedule, I don't get to aimlessly wander the malls as often as I'd like. Usually I go to get what I need and leave. But in the past month I have happened upon two, not one but two, days of pure bliss, where my husband was able to take time off work and take the kids for the day so I could relax. Relax and wander the mall, enjoying the serene bliss of moving at my own pace. Nowhere to be. No one to be responsible for. No one's happiness or entertainment to attend to except my own.

The mall is my version of meditation. A chance to get lost in my own thoughts, see what's hip and stylish so that I do not fall too far behind, people watch, and if I stumble upon something I deem glorious, buy something just for me – not because I need it but solely because I want it.

Now imagine that bliss being interrupted by BARK! BARK! GRRRRR!!! That's right, dogs barking and fighting. Startling me so much that I dropped the shoes I was handing to the sales person in Mecca, the Bloomingdale's shoe department. The sales person seemed nonplussed. Then another dog across from the shoe department over in DKNY started barking. Not a little toy dog carried by its overly stylish owner, but a big lab, lunging on its leash toward us. It heard the other dog. It smelled the other dog. Its animal instincts took over. The other little dog yapping uncontrollably by my sad pile of spilled shoes was going to be it's lunch. The owners were not doing much to calm them down – they were too busy with their own shopping to notice how they had disrupted mine. I left the Bloomingdales' shoes department, jumping as yet a third dog was tearing away at its leash, desperately trying to join the doggy barking/lunging/growling chorus happening on the second floor. Surely they wouldn't allow dogs on the third floor, in crystal and fine china. I was wrong. Little dogs on a leash. Big dogs on a leash. Dogs everywhere. When did the mall suddenly become a dog park?

The mall was once the bastion for young mothers. A safe place to stroll your buggy, let your child toddle about, meet up with other mothers to swap stories, and escape the doldrums of endless laundry and housework. Having been one of those mommy mall escapees, a child screaming or making noise I can zone out, but being assaulted by the growling and barking of someone's dog in a department store is just plain wrong. Not to mention it no longer makes it safe for the mommies and their little tots.

I truly figured that this was a fluke, that it had been so long since I wandered aimlessly that some cruel joke was being played upon me. Just my luck. So I felt that is why I had been given another chance. A week after the Bloomingdales' dog incident, on a glorious Southern California day, warm but breezy, the smell of fall in the air, the light slightly amber as the sun was now lower in the sky, I decided to spend the day with my mother at The Grove, a beautiful outdoor mall in Los Angeles, with wonderful shops and fabulous eateries with outdoor patios. A true shopping vacation day.

We ate a wonderful lunch and began to wander. And then it happened. We saw a woman shopping with a dog. One of those women who probably now bring their dogs with them everywhere. We skirted around her, and ducked into Nordstrom's. I love Nordstrom's. Everyone is so helpful. The sales associates and managers always go out of their way to make shopping a pleasant experience. Then the screeching of dogs began! In Nordstrom's! There, at the Bobbi Brown Makeup counter a woman was actually attempting to put on the new fall makeup line with two dogs pulling on leashes struggling to get away. She paid no attention to the fact that people were making a wide circle around her. That people were choosing not to shop in that aisle at all. She had no control over those dogs. They barked. They tangled themselves up in their leashes. They struggled to pull their owner to move, but she used all the muscle she could in her well manicured hand, not to allow them to pull her arm or hand away – she was applying the new fall colors to her face, after all.

That was it. Dogs in Nordstrom's? What has the shopping experience succumbed to?

What if the dogs had to poop? I doubt the lady struggling with her dogs at the makeup counter had plastic poop bags in her stylish but minute Prada handbag. What if they had to pee? Just go on the Nordstrom carpet – after all she was in the middle of finding a new lip color? What if they lunged at a kid and scared them to death? What if they bit a kid? Or an adult? What if they vomited from choking themselves on their collar? What if another customer tripped over them? Or slipped in the aisle on another dog's urine that had not been properly cleaned up? And who cleans it up? Next door at Ice, an accessory store, I asked a sales associate what was going on. She said they had to let them (the dogs and their owners) shop in the store. And the day before, a lady's dog threw up all over their floor. And then left. The sales associate was left to clean it up. Was that in her original job description? Wrong, wrong, wrong. I had a girlfriend whose kid threw up at a restaurant and then sat there and finished her meal as the hostess – with a hand over her nose, gloves on her hands, trying not to wretch herself cleaned up the puke at my friends feet. I was mortified. I should have demanded my friend clean up her own kid's puke, but I was frozen in shock and embarrassment at the situation. I still regret my behavior for allowing it. And that was a kid. I won't regret it again, not for a kid, not for a dog.

So my mother and I left Nordstrom's for their outdoor patio to take a break. We sat next to a young mother who was shopping with her own mother, and her new baby. It was beautiful and peaceful outside in the afternoon sun. Until, and I know this seems like it couldn't possible happen again, but a dog started barking from under a nearby table. Which set off another dog further down the courtyard. The young mother jumped up to protect her sleeping baby. My instincts flare up to protect my mother and myself. The people with the dogs saw our startled reactions. No apology. No shushing of their dogs. No dog etiquette, whatsoever. So what is dog store etiquette? I decided to find out for myself.

A senior customer service manager at the Bloomingdales in Sherman Oaks told me, "We're able to have people bring dogs in as long as they don't pose a threat. It's a liberal policy. We won't advertise it, but we won't ask them to leave. We are a high-end store and our clientele thinks of their dogs as children. If you are uncomfortable, please tell a manager, we don't want dogs to make our guests or their children (human I assumed) uncomfortable."

How will you know if the dogs pose a threat until they become a threat? I don't know. They don't know either. The truth is if you are going to compare the dogs to children, let's get down to basics. Dogs, like small children squirming in their mothers' arms or strollers, don't want to be at the mall while the adults dilly dally shopping. They are bored. They want to run. They want to play. They want your undivided attention. And we all know that with all the glorious displays begging to be seen, touched and purchased at the stores, your attention is sure to be divided and constantly diverted.

So take them - your dogs - to the park. But please, make sure it's a dog park...

My Word

After lunch with new friends we all stepped out into the chilly air to say our goodbyes. Putting on our coats, one new friend said to me, "You look smart!" "That's an old fashioned word. Thanks, it's a new coat," I replied as I tightened my coat belt for effect. "No," she said slowly, deliberately and with some surprise, "you look 'smart smart'." In a minor state of shock, I stood there speechless as my new friends sized ME up - not just my fabulous new coat. Quickly assessing the situation and gathering my wits, I replied with more than a hint of sarcasm, "Well! I am not just another pretty face!" The laughter at the retort broke the awkward moment and we parted ways with the promise to get together again soon. But I walked away wondering, "Do I not strike people as 'smart smart'?"

Two days later I received a junk email from a different acquaintance. Sometimes these are funny, sometimes not, but if I have the time I like to play along. This particular email asked all her friends to send back just one adjective describing her. Obviously just a feel good email, but as is my custom I put some thought and energy into it. I came up with a couple words but they did not feel right. I consulted my thesaurus, my dictionary and finally emailed her back her word, "generous." This is a word loaded with meaning - descriptive and action oriented and I felt I truly matched many facets of her personality and who she strove to be as a person.

I ran into her later that same day, and I happened to be wearing my new coat. She spoke loudly, as there were many people and several tables separating us, "I got my word! I loved it!" she shouted." Do you want to know what yours is?" This took me off guard. I had not forwarded the request to any of 'my people', for although I was curious and would have enjoyed it, I am very selective of the junk emails I send and for one reason or another this one did not pass the selection process. But I digress. So I'm standing on the other side of the tables and she is shouting from hers, surrounded by several other people and I stop in mid stride and turn to face them all. "Okay," I say, sounding like the meek about to be judged (yet another reason I did not forward it – I hate to put myself in this position). But she was sooooo enthusiastic and wanted to give me my word – she is 'generous' after all. So I stood there, facing my judges. She smiles and shouts, "Beautiful! That's your word." Then she turns to her friends. "Isn't she beautiful? She always looks so nice." She, and the people I barely knew stood there waiting for a reply – my reply. So I smiled beautifully and waved beautifully and walked beautifully away. She hollered again after me, "You're beautiful!" And this was for some reason more than I could take (odd, I know as she was truly being 'generous' and nice) but I could not stop myself from blurting, "I am not just beautiful! I am smart." I once again tightened the belt on my jacket for effect, smiled and walked on.

Events that throw me off kilter always come back in odd and often inappropriate ways, catching me off guard. But they do usually teach me something about myself, and/or the world in which I live. Why was I so disappointed in her word? Disappointed enough to make a bit of a scene to refute it? Maybe because I had actually consulted a dictionary and thesaurus to come up with a word that would fit many facets of who she was? Or maybe because I see myself as so much more than others see me. Or maybe because I'm surprised at the way others don't see me....

So how do I see myself? How do others really see me? And what is my word? I feel an urgent need to choose my own appropriate adjective. And then I realize it may have been chosen for me. By new friends who sized me up immediately. "Smart." I am smart. I am 'smart smart'. I am smart looking. I have a smart wit about me. I dress smartly. I have a smart set of friends. I could go on and on. What a truly great word! It's an adjective, it's a noun, it's an adverb, it's a verb. This word encompasses many facets of my personality. Smart is now MY word. And while we are all many things, many adjectives, the exercise of choosing just one to describe you can prove to be a smart journey.

Grace

"What is grace?" A seven year-old I know quite well, turned his inquisitive face to me and asked after I suggested he lead grace at the dinner table. I looked, evidently a bit shocked, to his mother who quickly quipped, "We do not worship in our house. You can say grace if you want."

I wasn't sure what to say. I don't think of grace as worship. I don't think of it as belonging to any faith. This was not a religious holiday gathering, but it was a time to be thankful, grateful. We don't do it every meal, but in my family we often go around the dinner table and say something about our day or someone opts to lead grace, whatever that means for him or her in that moment. So I asked around in my very "melting pot" circle of friends and colleagues. Some people do say thanks or blessings before a meal, some don't, but almost all felt that grace was a religious term.

Surprised by my mini poll results, I turned to the most reliable source I know – The Dictionary. In the dictionary "grace" is defined many ways, yes some referring to God, but the top tier definitions, the ones that came first before any religious connotations were: a dignified, polite, and decent behavior; and a capacity to tolerate, accommodate or forgive people.

I had to go back and read the definitions again. Polite. Accommodating. Forgiving. Dignified. Tolerant. These are characteristics we all strive for, aren't they? Especially where we live, in Los Angeles, where I hear at least four languages on a daily basis and where my kids see no color or faith when choosing their friends. Even in our community we come across situations where grace is desperately needed: in front of the school during pickup time, at the mall during the holiday rush, on the freeway, in line at the coffee shop.

I want my kids, and your kids, to be grateful, thankful for what they have and to realize that not everyone is so lucky. I even want them to find the motivation on their own to help others. I want them to be respectful, accommodating and tolerant of other people's traditions. I want the adults to be polite and dignified in the way they talk about other peoples' celebrations, knowing that what they say gets passed on through their children to my and other children.

Thanksgiving (and anytime throughout the year) can be about embracing grace, no matter what you believe in. For with grace, we can hopefully build a wonderful community in which to raise decent, polite, tolerant, dignified and forgiving children.

Kendall learns much from his very graceful grandmother, Nona.

Silence Validates

Please help! I am losing the "But, Mom, they're doing it! Why did she do/say that to me?" battle. It's endless. I've explained that every household has different rules, and someone else doing it does not make it okay for them. But this argument is being challenged daily. And not just by the kids. Children are witnessing you, the parents, ignoring or blatantly defying the rules that govern our society. They point it out. They talk about it. And when I, or another adult, call you on it, a verbal assault of expletives often follows. Which leads to yet another conversation not just about inappropriate actions but about inappropriate reactions and bad language as well. It is a vicious cycle.

Trying to decide what, when and if to say something is increasingly more difficult. People are becoming afraid to speak up, and the silence of no one saying anything validates the offending behavior. Which leads to more atrocious "the world revolves around me" conduct.

It is our children who don't understand the silence and keep breaking it. They ask the questions we should be asking. "Why? What?" Because if kids don't witness repercussions for behavior, then they will no longer abide by the rules. Where are the boundaries? What are the consequences?"

And yes, I am talking about the dangerous driving and illegal parking. But I am also talking about the behavior toward other human beings. The things you say to (or in front of) your kids about the way another adult or child looks, the name-calling, and negative comments about their race or religious celebrations that (of course!) get back to other children at school. It is rampant.

So, through their tears, when my or any child asks me why they were treated so poorly by another child, I may sadly say, "Those kids behave that way because their parents do. Or because their parents let them get away with it." I implore you, please pay attention to the behavior, the boundaries and the consequences. When you don't it makes life difficult for everyone in this society that we call home.

The BEST Gift for Kids Is evidently NOT a THING.

My kids don't remember what they got last Christmas. I can't begin to tell how this irritates me. When pushed they remember getting one Yu-Gi-Oh pack. Safe guess. They get one of those regularly. The amount of time, energy and money put into getting them what they would actually use, treasure even, was, evidently, wasted. Even Santa's gifts weren't remembered. At least my efforts are not outranked by Santa's. I try to keep this in mind as I frantically look online for the one gift I think they want this year but is sold out everywhere. At least if I can't find it, I now know they ultimately won't remember. Oddly, there is little consolation in that for me.

So what do they remember? After almost a half hour of prodding them to remember what they had received last year, they started talking about the things we DID. "You know, our Traditions," said Kendall. Wow. I was speechless.

I did not have any real traditions in my family growing up. No extended family either. So it was important to me to create that for my kids. I was always envious of my friends who had what seemed to me cultural or family traditions. I always felt this defined them somehow, and that I lacked that definition, that community. So as an adult and a mother it was important to me to establish a sense of identity for my kids – through extended family and traditions. I did not know until now that I had succeeded.

"I love the musical caroling," said Kamden. Both sides of our family, grandparents, aunts, uncles, and cousins come to our house on Christmas Eve where we eat Italian food (this was a random choice on my part for no one in our family is Italian) grab an instrument and go caroling to our neighbors. Our neighbors have already asked us if they can expect us this year. Evidently, this is now an official Tradition for them as well.

The Paper Roll Fight is Kendall's favorite. He asked if I had already started collecting empty wrapping paper rolls. I tell him, yes, but that I don't have many yet. "Well, you better let everyone know you need some." On Christmas Day, after the gifts are all opened, everyone goes outside and grabs an empty roll from a bucket holding many empty rolls. Young and old, we commence a paper roll fight. I have rarely seen my mom, their Grammy, laugh so loud or try so hard to win year after year. For it is the last person standing with an intact paper roll that wins the "prize". Oddly, my kids did remember this gift from last year, a digital clock – perhaps because they didn't win it, their Uncle John did.

I was so moved and elated that this is what they remember about their Holiday and curious as to what other Traditions defined Christmas for them. They quickly rattled them off:

"Going to the top of Reseda, drinking hot cider, and looking for Rudolph and Santa's Sleigh!" We have seen it every year.

"Tamales to eat on Christmas Day!" I borrowed Traditions from all cultures, this one stuck.

"The Magic Box Unwrapping Game." This is a bit like musical chairs, but you must unwrap a box as fast as you can until the music starts again. Once the music starts you pass it around. The person who unwraps it completely keeps it. This is actually a new Tradition started last year by their Aunt Ricki.

"Dada dressing up as Santa!" This started the year after I found a fabulous Santa suit at Restoration Hardware on clearance.

"Leaving carrots out for the Reindeer and cookies for Santa." Carrot pieces are invariably strewn about our yard. Reindeer get hungry, too.

"Decorating the House and The Christmas Village." This year I hope they don't notice we didn't do the Christmas Village. I feel guilty about it, but it takes soooo long.

"Going to Candy Cane Lane." We all love seeing the giant Santa and beautifully decorated homes in the area between Corbin and Winnetka north of the 101. Where do those people store all those massive decorations? That is a true traditions and huge commitment.

The list kept going on for a while as we lay in bed and talked about all the fun times we have had over Christmases Past. "What do you think will be the best part of Christmas this year?" I asked. We were all silent. Thinking to ourselves what that might be. At least at that moment I knew they were not thinking of a video game machine or skate shoes. I knew they were thinking of their family and the lasting memories we would create together in a few weeks' time.

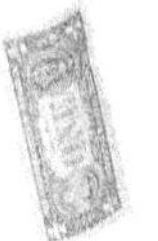

From the Mouths of Babes

Kids say the scrappiest things.

They speak the truth.

Most of the time.

Regardless of consequence.

And that is what makes what they say so valuable.

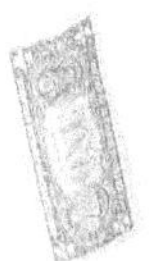

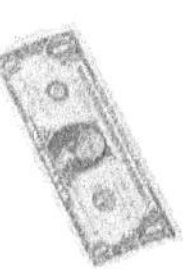

Scraps

When life gets crazy, something has to give. In my life, that something has evidently been me. This realization just hit me like a ton a bricks. After making burritos with fresh grown cilantro for my kids, I was cleaning up the kitchen, on the phone taking care of business, and signing school papers all at once. Although hungry, I was unable to actually sit and eat with my kids because I was "too busy." Kendall got up from the table and went to scrape his plate, stopped himself and turned to me, "Do you want my scraps," he asked holding his plate over the trash, waiting for my answer.

Of course, I did. But his innocent question kept coming back into my head over the next several days. And it really bothered me. While from his perspective he was trying to do something for me, the more I thought about what the whole situation actually meant, the more depressed I became. I do so much for my kids and for others that there has been no time to do anything for me. I literally get the scraps. I haven't been able to eat properly – only what's left on my kids' plate. I haven't had time to exercise – not even to walk my dog. My hair is in desperate need of a cut and color, while my kids' hair is neat and trimmed. My oldest and I are redecorating his room into a 'big boy' room – again. It has already been painted and done once. My room never has. The original nail holes and markings from the previous owner are still on my walls. I see them everyday. Everyday for eight and a half years. And my marriage. Talk about something that gets only the leftover scraps.

I realize during this self-reflection that things have to shift. Life has changed a lot for me and for my family over the past year, mostly good changes, but some things have suffered. Things that used to be of the utmost importance have slipped. And it's starting to show. During my favorite morning snuggle time, my son told me my arm feels different. This didn't register at first. He didn't say it in a mean way. But later, after getting on the scale for the first time in four months I saw what he meant. I was up ten pounds! This of course, was extremely shocking – I eat only scraps after all. But, evidently, that has taken its toll. Whereas eating right, eating together, exercising on my own and with my kids – I was a volunteer PE coach for both kids' classes - used to be a big part of my life, it has all taken a back seat. And my kids can tell. Not just by how my arms feel, I realize sadly, but my presence, or lack thereof. I also feel the change as I realize I miss them terribly when they are at a friend's house, whereas that used to be a much-needed reprieve.

So this balancing act, a struggle faced everyday, has become more difficult for me. What is important? Where should each item be on the time allotment scale? And how do I find a way to balance it? I chose to figure it out in a way that has worked in the past. I'll make a list and chart. I've done it for my kids a million times. It works for them, it'll work for me. A list I can check off everyday. My accountability list. Eat right. Exercise. Vitamins. Walk the Dog. Volunteer at school. Coach PE. Make time to sit with my husband and get to know each other again. Do nails. Wash Face. Apply good cream. Breathe.

"Breathe" resonates the most. Perhaps because in my past, during other challenging times, post-its and note cards with just that one word have been prominently displayed. Now, once again, I stick it everywhere I am sure to see it. In the car. In the kitchen. On my keychain. I will make time to breathe. I will make time for what is important. I will get more out of life than just the scraps.

Time For It

Cleaning out my kid's backpack I pulled out what looked like a homework assignment. The paper, which I read aloud, instructed him to lie down in the grass, eyes closed, and listen to the sounds, feel the air, smell the smells, then write about his experience. "Wow," I said, "how great! Let's make sure we do that." My 6-year-old then said matter-of-factly, "We just don't have time. It's extra credit." Suddenly my baby seemed older. Like a little man. And in this moment I felt sad and proud and frustrated. Sad that at 6 he doesn't feel that he has time to lie in the grass and experience what our backyard has to offer his senses. Sad that it was true we could not stop our lives at that moment to do this task. But I was proud that he was being responsible in prioritizing his activities. Proud that he was managing time. And frustrated that at the tender age of 6 this was all going on in his gorgeous little head. Frustrated that although I strive to give my kids a balanced life, we just don't have time to stop our day and lie in the grass. My kids aren't overscheduled. I don't believe in multiple sports and planned activities or classes everyday. I want my boys to run like banshees with their friends on the playground or have a play date where they use their imaginations to become the next great scientist or quarterback of the Rose Bowl. And yet, nine days have passed since I first saw that paper and we have yet to lie in the grass. Why can't we do it? Why can't we stop and just lay in the grass? You'd think the weekends would be the perfect time, but between traveling soccer tournaments, birthday parties, chores and errands, our time on the grass keeps getting pushed back. But we cannot throw that paper out. We leave it there and talk about it almost daily. We laugh about it. We discuss it and our days and ways to make it happen. So even though we have not actually dropped everything to go outside and lie in the grass, this piece of paper is helping us to connect at the end of each day. It has become a touchpoint for me and my kids to discuss what is going on in their worlds. This paper, and it's ever pending activity, has given me an avenue to become closer to my kids, to learn more about their values and priorities. And one day, we will go outside and lie in the grass. But not until I know for sure that this laughter and conversation will continue on once we do – for this has become more than just a one night extra credit assignment, this has become part of our daily routine. And yes, we have somehow made time for it.

Routine Treasures

As I had done everyday for the past 160 days of school, I walked my son into his classroom and hugged and kissed him goodbye. His body froze. His face turned into a grumpy scowl. Then I asked the question whose answer a mother is never prepared for. "What is it?" "You are embarrassing me!" he hissed slowly through clenched teeth so his friends would not hear.

I was stunned. I felt like someone slapped me in the face. Literally speechless. I didn't even notice that I had raised my hand and asked for a high five. But I did notice when he grabbed my finger hard, bringing my hand down. "Y-o-u a-r-e e-m-b-a-r-a-s-s-i-n-g m-e!" he said again so slowly that I felt like I was in a time warp.

Boy did it sink in that time. My heart felt tight and dropped to my stomach. I felt sick. My face flushed. I tried to smile and wave. I tried to tell him I loved him and to have a great day. Over and over. Trying to get a response. I was like a fish floundering painfully outside its fish bowl. "Someone give me some water!" But he didn't. No looking back. Realizing I was doing more damage than repair at this point, I left the room in a daze, choking back my tears.

It was at this moment that I realized I needed him more than he needed me. That I had raised an independent self assured young man who feels safe enough to separate from me and venture out on his own. And even though I wasn't ready, he was. Stumbling back to my car I bumped (literally) into a friend and through choked back tears told her what happened. She gave me a hug and told me the same thing happened to her last year when her son entered the seventh grade. I pulled away. Looked at her. "This is his last week of Kindergarten!" I wanted to yell. "Not seventh grade! I want seventh grade!" But I didn't yell. I walked away. Alone.

Two days and two torturous 'grown up' good-byes later he wanted me to sit next to him on the bus for a field trip. "Really?!" I asked feeling like I was the child and he the parent. "It's okay if you sit with your friends." But my little just-turned-six-year-old insisted that I was his chosen seat partner. I felt as though the angels were singing a chorus of beautiful voices around us as he excitedly took my hand and said, "You're sitting next to me." Wow. Time flies. And fluctuates. And the seemingly mundane daily routines are the moments I've learned to treasure.

Bonus Moment

We have all heard it said that being a mom is a thankless job. There are no reviews, no raises, no monetary bonuses tied to our performance.

But occasionally moments happen that are more valuable than any bonus or raise. These moments bring you to tears, acknowledge, and validate all the love and sacrifices you have made for your children. These moments give you thanks.

One such moment for me happened over Spring Break. After years of my kids 'proving' they were ready, we finally brought home a puppy. My boys were overjoyed, but they also showed a calm maturity beyond their years - with the gentle tenderness and the unconditional love and care they showed our puppy. "My little darling" is what my seven year old called her from the moment he met her. Stroking her, teaching her, caring for her, cleaning up after her, making sure she felt safe in her new surroundings.

My nine year old had read several books on puppies and was more than adequately prepared to make sure all was handled appropriately - what she needed, the training to begin right away, what her behaviors signified she needed from us. His strong confident behavior, his patience and the love from both of them was overwhelming....

Watching my boys love and appropriately care for another living creature allowed me a glimpse of the men they would become....of the kind of fathers they would one day be. My heart welled, my eyes teared up. This was my bonus moment, my review, where it was shown to me that I have raised two really wonderful human beings.

True Friends

"Who is your best friend?" My son recently asked me. His intensity caught me a bit off guard. I haven't heard that question since I was in school, and the person asking wanted to make sure the answer was her name – because back then, we all had one and only one best friend.

"I don't have just one," I finally replied (feeling all grown-up), "I have several."

"But you have to choose just one person," he persisted. At this point I could feel his internal struggle. This wasn't just idle conversation. "Do you have a best friend?" I asked. Both of my boys became entrenched in getting to the bottom of this for everyone and a lively discussion ensued.

"It is so hard to pick just one," they both agreed, pleadingly, looking to me for the answer. "So don't," I said, the pain of not being chosen and the elation of knowing you've been chosen came flooding back. How do I save them from this? "But you have to!" They insisted. So I took a deep breath.

I struggled to find the right words. "There will be a lot of wonderful friends who come into your life," I began, "and depending on what's going on at that particular time, you will feel more connected to certain friends than others."

"Like my new friends this year that used to be my old friends when I was younger?" They asked. "Or my friends I had last year that I don't really play with this year?" "And my new friend in my class that I really like?"

They were getting it. I smiled, nodded and continued, thinking of my own friends.

I tried to explain that it isn't one best friend that they are seeking. It is a true friend. Best friends change, come and go. But a true friend will be there for you, even when they are not your current "best friend." A true friend will be the one cheering for you, congratulating you, and being happy for you, even when your "best friend" is no where to be found. A true friend will be the one who is not laughing when you embarrass yourself – and laughs with you when you are ready. A true friend will be the one that you can always sit with at lunch, even if you have not spoken for a while. A true friend is someone you know is there, regardless, even after you disagree, argue or fight. A true friend lets you be you. A true friend is where you feel safe.

"So a true friend is like family," my youngest asked. I couldn't have said it better. And in that moment I could see that they knew in their hearts who their true friends were.

Pay Attention To Life!

A few days ago, I took part in a business meeting in a very beige corporate conference room along with two owners of the company, their technical adviser, and a colleague of mine. During what I (erroneously) thought was an engaging conversation, one man answered his cell phone and had a full conversation without moving away (no one commented on how rude this was), another regularly looked down to spin the wheel on his blackberry, and yet another kept walking away and coming back to loudly interject his opinion to whatever he supposed we were still talking about – as though he were an active and important part of the conversation. This behavior made me feel about as important as a squished ant.

There was no respect for the moment, for the people who were actually right in front of them.

As horrified and appalled as I was at this behavior, I didn't do anything about it because I didn't know how to appropriately respond to it. It was my son who presented me with the answer to this issue. We – my whole family - were all engrossed in our own madness that is daily life, when my seven year-old, Kamden, blurted out in frustration what has since become a family motto, "Pay attention to life!"

The commanding tone in his voice startled me. His words caught me off guard. And the desperation he conveyed to actually be listened to, to actually be paid attention to - one hundred percent, spoke volumes to a basic need in all of us, a need that we fight for everyday. I was startled. Had I made him feel like a squished ant, too?

Do you, really, pay attention to the moment? Or are you busy planning the next or regretting the last? I have found that it is much more difficult to actually experience life, to pay attention to it as it happens, than it is to plan it.

After Kamden's outburst, the words stuck with me. Constantly, I found myself in situations where I wanted to blurt out my family's new motto. I've now noticed how often this lack of "living in the moment" happens in daily life. From the way people drive, to people you say hello to that don't even see you, to the sales clerk who lets you stand and wait while they answer the telephone and fulfill the requests of those individuals who did not make the effort to actually come into the store. The more I think about it, the more offended at others behavior and yet possibly embarrassed at my own behavior I become. How many times had my kids, or someone else, been in front of me that I did not give the moment to?

Now that I am actually trying to pay attention to life, I realize I usually don't. Multitasking, planning, preparing, worrying, these all take me out of the present and plunk me in the past and/or the future. Time is too precious! My kids are growing up so fast, I don't want to look back and realize my head and attention were always somewhere else!

Paying attention to life is not always easy. Or possible. But it is important. For you, for me, for all of us. This lesson, a lesson from my young son, I now carry with me. Kamden demanded we all pay attention to life, and in that moment, we all did.

Like You

Birthdays are a big deal in our household. Just as big if not bigger than any other holiday. It is a day all to yourself, to be celebrated just for being you. Cake and ice cream for breakfast. Taken out to lunch. A special dinner of your choosing with more deserts and gifts.

This year for my birthday my husband was out of the country. The kids knew my birthday was coming up, but truly, it could have passed unnoticed for me (how boring to be 29, again!). But on October 12, my two kids woke me up with sweet snuggles and birthday wishes. They showed off the fact they were dressed and their beds made.

As we headed downstairs I could tell by their hurried steps and constant glances and smiles that something was up. With a bit of a "ta-da!" on their part, I entered the kitchen. There before me, my daily breakfast of a bowl of cheerios, cup of yogurt and glass of water were beautifully placed at what is now 'my spot' at the table – complete with napkin and silverware. Surrounding the setting were the most beautifully crafted three-dimensional cards with 'Happy Birthday' and 'I love you Mom' written in various sections on them.

My oldest pulled out my chair for me to sit down. They sat on my lap as I ate. They both had already eaten, you see. They had set their alarms for 5:30am and had been up since then getting everything ready for me as a surprise. I gazed at them, all choked up with emotion, unable to eat my cheerios. This they didn't understand, for I never skip breakfast! I gave them each a big hug and told them how special this gesture was to me. That it was the best birthday gift ever. Hopping off my lap, they refilled my glass, made their own lunches (gasp!), fed the dog, packed the car and got in ready to go. I didn't have to do a thing. No clean up - they did it. No hollering about hurrying up - they were ready. We actually made it to school before the gates were open. It was the easiest, most relaxed school morning I believe I've ever had. I kissed them good-bye at the gate and was in a glorious daze, smiling to myself, all day long.

At dinner, they asked if I had had a good day. "Stupendous!" I replied, always trying to incorporate their spelling words into our daily conversations, "especially after your wonderful surprise this morning." "Well," they answered, "we wanted to do something special like you do for us. Like you do. Everyday. Like you, Mom."

The Family That Plays Together....

Sometimes, you have to dig through the pile of scraps to find the morsel with just enough sustenance on it to nourish you.

This is what maintaining family life can feel like in our society today.

But nothing is better than the savory little piece you discover when you least expect it.

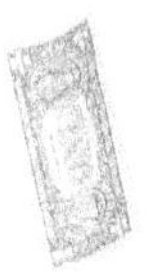

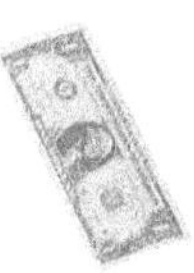

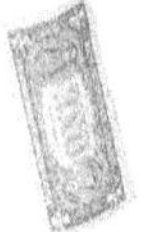

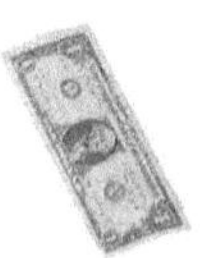

Oscars are the Ultimate Prom Night

Getting ready for and attending the Academy Awards can only be likened to going to the Prom. Seriously. After the initial excitement of actually being able to attend such a glamorous event, my first thought was, of course, what would I wear? My second thought was, what will everyone else be wearing? I bought a few magazines, looked at the latest styles, logged on to some websites that held the promise of Oscar fashion previews and finally just retired to my bed too overwhelmed by the thought of preparing for the whole experience. Men have it so easy. Double or single-breasted tux? And it's a rental. And it comes with shoes. Shoes! Good lord, where would I begin to look for shoes? And how could I begin to look until I found a dress? And what would I do with my hair?

I honestly felt like I was in high school, again. Not a period of time I ever wanted to revisit. So I decided to let it go. To just wear something I already had. Then my mom called. "You most certainly will not!" she exclaimed when I told her of my plan. Two days later she came to L.A. and we spent an entire afternoon searching for and finding a dress and shoes. No time left for jewelry, but by the end of the day, I felt confident I could do that on my own. It was really fun. I hadn't been shopping with my mom for an 'important' dress since my wedding. And my mom does not share my love of high heels, so I was surprised by her enthusiasm in choosing such glitzy ones. The dress was perfect. Colorful with just the right amount of beading to give it the necessary glamour. And the sales associate at All

Dressed Up in Reseda, where we found my gown, indicated to my mom that it did not make me look like a sausage. Yeah, she was a wonderful saleswoman. Still, she got the sale, and my mom insisted upon buying it. I think it was her way of ensuring that a little bit of her would be able to experience the Oscars with me.

So with the dress and shoes hanging proudly in my room, I was able to focus on hair and make-up. My hair stylist of ten years was unavailable so I had to search for someone new. Oddly, this was much more stressful than searching for a dress that would not make me look like a sausage. First of all, the Oscars are on a Sunday. Most hair salons are closed on Sundays. And none were willing to open just for me. That put me in my place. Just going to the Oscars is not such a big deal to other people. Welcome to L.A. I finally found a place in the Sherman Oaks Fashion Square. The young man had time on Sunday morning, so I booked it. My mom came in early that day to go with me. Honestly, it was like she was going instead of me. Still, it was great having her there. The stylist did my hair in an updo that was so tight and painful I had to have him take it out and redo it. In the end, it was okay, but now I know why movie stars find a stylist they like and put them on staff – so they can count on them when they really need them. Still, if I could, I would hire a cook first. But I digress in my financial fantasy.

Once home from being professionally coiffed, I dressed, applied a bit more makeup than usual and descended the stairs. My two boys, my husband (and my date), my mom, my sister, her two daughters and her son were all ooohhing and aaahhhhing around me. I felt like a real princess. Alas, there was no tiara or chariot, only my fine Chrysler Town and Country, but at least it was shiny and clean. Yes, I went to the Oscars in a minivan.

Driving in on the 101 to Cahuenga, we came upon Hollywood Boulevard, which, on this night, we needed to show our special car pass to even access this area. All of a sudden we felt like kids at Disneyland for the first time. The anticipation and excitement got the better of both of us. Hundreds of people line up along this stretch of Hollywood Boulevard, trying to get a look at those that are able to pass, taking our picture even, just in case we are Hollywood players (did they not notice the minivan?) Scores and scores of police surround this area and we were forced to weave our car in and out of concrete pylons and through an official check point before coming up to the valet who took our car right there in front of the entrance to the red carpet.

The lights illuminating the Kodak Theatre and the entrance to the red carpet make everyone look good. The Hollywood magic starts here. Standing on the carpet, surrounded by glittering larger than life Oscars, and looking up into the screaming faces of thousands of fans hoping to get a glimpse of their favorite movie star. I suddenly felt like I had gone back in time to old Hollywood. I was here, at the Academy Awards.

The red carpet experience is amazing. Walking slowly along the ropes, stars, Hollywood mucky mucks, and Hollywood not so mucky mucks surrounded me, but still I wondered whom each person was that I passed, or accidentally bumped into, as it was wonderfully crowded. How did they get here? The gowns were beautiful. It was like swimming in a stream of fine fabric and couture. The stars and mere attendees alike did all they could to show off what they had painstaking chosen to adorn themselves in. The long trains that many women wore were constantly being stepped on. Surprisingly, no one got angry, it was just part of the experience. The jewels on my fancy new shoes kept catching on the bottom of my dress. I knew that the shoes or the dress would be ruined by evening's end, which I realized is why no one ever wears the same gown twice - because it will have been mauled by the crowds and stepped on and abused and it's lucky it survives this one night.

Inside the Kodak Theatre, waiters float about offering delicious hors d'oevres made by Wolfgang Puck. The bar is crowded and the booze flows freely. I wanted to explore, so we made our way down to the lower level to mingle. I can liken this experience only to being at a cocktail party where you feel like you know everyone. We stood at the bar next to Nicole Kidman. We said hello. She is even more gorgeous and flawless in person. In another room, we made small talk with Sting and Trudy, said hello to Jamie Lee Curtis who said hello back as we passed each other getting on and off the elevator. Oprah whisked by us, and everyone smiled at everyone and we smiled back. At this point I wasn't sure whom I knew and who I thought I knew, but didn't actually know. A woman came up to me and said hello. Did I know her? Or was she a movie star? Turns out I had met her at a Southern Living party at a friend's house. I saw an old boss and another ancillary acquaintance. After a while, I just started talking to everyone because everyone was so familiar - albeit for different reasons. It was glorious and fun and I felt right at home and had no problems fitting in. Several women actually even commented on my gown and how lovely it was. I wanted to tell them I chose it all on my own, without a stylist, but I didn't as I didn't want to give the illusion of who I might be (or might not be) away.

Once the show started we made our way up the stairs to the balcony. It was a wonderful show to actually experience live. During the commercial breaks, the cocktail atmosphere continued until the "10 seconds to air" announcement came, at which point everyone scurried back into their seats. Yes, everyone. The show was also long (just like it is at home), and sitting in a gown does start to make one feel like the dreaded sausage the lady at the dress store spoke of. At the end of the show, everyone from all levels exit through the main doors. Literally a huge crowd of stars, producers, directors, and ordinary folk like me are funneled together in the lobby through large glass doors. Hmm, I thought, they have to exit the same way we do. I don't know why this was so interesting to me, we all entered from the red carpet, after all.

More gowns were stepped on, some even torn. But everyone maintained their dignity and held their heads high, smiling and congratulating those they came into contact with in this flowing sea of Hollywood royalty. When we eventually made it out, I looked back to take in one last glimpse. It was a magical evening, much better than my senior prom. But like my prom night, I could hear the clock striking midnight and realized it was time to return home, for my mom and dad were once again waiting up for me, although for a very different reason than twenty years ago. They were babysitting my kids for whom I am a star everyday.

Bathroom Mission Adventure

I am having bathroom issues and I do not know how to consistently and appropriately handle it. I do the best I can in each situation, but on occasion, some people get offended, I feel awkward and/or a fight ensues between my two boys and me. Let me explain.

Are you from Southern California or did your kids grow up here? Do you remember doing a mission report in 4th grade? Nearly everyone I talk to does or has already been through it with their kids. "Ah, the fourth grade mission project," they all say (in varying tones of fondness and 'poor you'). My sister remembers. She still has her miniature mission project that our grandfather helped her build in the garage of our parents' house. As shocking as this should be, it's not. There hasn't been a car in that garage since the 1970's. (Thanks, Mom, for saving everything, really!)

Growing up in Southern California, the mission report is, and has been for some time, part of the standard curriculum. That I personally don't remember it does not surprise me. I did not enjoy history as a kid. It was taught out of a book, with lots of facts, names and dates to memorize. There was nothing in my life, no experiences that I could link it to, so it didn't stick. Which is why I try to make history interesting for my kids, so that it will stick, so that it will have meaning for them.

So when Kendall was assigned a mission, the Mission San Carlos Borromeo del Rio Carmelo, in Carmel, California, I decided we should go see it. Experience it. Touch it. Witness the history of California first hand. That it was in Carmel was a bonus, an excuse, really, for a mother – son adventure.

We set off on the Saturday morning of a three-day weekend. I hadn't prepared myself for the holiday traffic, and neither had MapQuest – my printout said it would only take five hours to get there. After about 4 and a half hours of traffic we had to stop to go to the bathroom. I saw a Wal-Mart off the 101. We pulled off and went in. A grumpy old man hollered at my kids not to skate in the store (we had literally just walked in the store, or in their case, wheeled in on their Heely's). I looked at him and said, "Please," as though I were instructing a child on how to appropriately behave. Kids deserve the same respect adults do. We all walked (not wheeled) the 10 feet to the bathroom. And that is when we all paused. Here it was again. The awkward fight. The pleading from my sons' eyes. Finally my oldest said it, "I would rather not go than have to go in the women's room." And he meant it. He is stubborn as can be (I have no idea where he gets that from). So I stood there. It was then I noticed two other women standing at the door of the men's bathroom. "Okay," I agreed reluctantly, "you and your brother go in together and come out together. If you're not out in 30 seconds, I'm coming in." They smiled in relief – they wouldn't have to 'hold-it' - and raced into the bathroom.

The other two women waiting outside the door were very different from me. They had a lot of tattoos, photo jewelry and piercings, but in this instance we were all of the same group – mothers worried about their boys going into the men's room. We compared experiences (they had a lot more than I did) and they told me horror stories.

At that moment, a man walked up to the door. We were quite a sight, I'm sure, three women blocking the door to the men's room. He didn't know what to do. He started to go in. I couldn't take it! "Our children are in there. They'll be out in a minute – thanks for understanding, and for waiting." He had obviously never been asked this before and he started to say something. But there we were, three Mama bears protecting their cubs. What could he possibly say? So he stepped back and waited. The women and I parted ways after our kids came out, and I will most likely never see them again in my life. But I will always remember them. For we shared a common bond in that moment. In that moment we were the same. As my kids wheeled on their shoes back to the car, I told them not to get used to that – that they would still have to go in the women's restroom with me, sometimes. "I would rather go in my pants," my oldest said. Great. I knew he meant it.

We finally arrived at our hotel in Carmel. It was old, but very clean and roomy enough for me and my two boys. They literally started bouncing off the walls and the beds the moment we arrived – it was a long journey in a car for them. After they expelled a bit of energy, we reluctantly got back in the car to seek out the Mission and get some food. The hotel was right off Highway 1 and the office clerk was very friendly and offered maps and directions. It was very dark – I am used to street lamps everywhere illuminating the night, but after passing the mission, my youngest, Kamden spotted it on our way back. We did not stop – it was late and dark and we were all hungry. But we also felt better knowing that we knew how to get to it first thing in the morning. We ate a hearty meal at the Black Bear Diner - a northern California franchise – and settled back into our room. "It's amazing how tired I am from sitting in the car all day," Kamden said just before falling asleep.

We spent the next day exploring the mission. Kendall and Kamden loved it. We even went to mass (bonus points for me). Kendall was fascinated to see in person things he had only read and learned about in school. So far, the trip had been worth every penny.

After the mission, we headed off to the Monterey Bay Aquarium. Many, many times by different people, I had been told how fabulous this aquarium was. We waited in line for about a half an hour just to buy tickets. Then walked inside and saw the thousands of other people who had waited in line before us. And this time, I had to go to the bathroom. I asked at the information desk where the bathroom was (it was too crowded to try and wander and find it on my own). I approached the women's sign with trepidation. "Do you have to go?" I asked my boys. Two darling heads shook no – and four eyes indicated they would not be going in with me. I put them against the wall right outside the bathroom. I looked around. Hundreds and hundreds of people. Strangers. Do I make a scene and force them to come in with me? "If anyone approaches you, yell as loud as you can and make a scene!" I instructed them – they were all for it. I went in, feeling anxious. There was a line. A long line. I really had to go! But, I just could not leave my two boys outside this bathroom unattended while I waited in line. I left, ready to leave the museum (it was not worth the $56.85 to get in to go through that anxiety).

But then I saw an escalator. And went up. I was on a mission. Fewer people were upstairs, and the further back we went, the less people we encountered. Finally a bathroom sign emerged. Thank you! There were not a lot of people. Mostly mom's with babies, as this bathroom happened to be right by the kiddie play area of the aquarium. "Stay here," I said as I pushed their backs up against the wall right outside the bathroom, 'and scream loudly, 'this is not my mother, this is not my father,' if anyone approaches you. I ran in, did my business and ran out. They were fine. But I was a mess. When will this get easier, when will I be comfortable with this?

I knew then as we walked away from that bathroom that I would be facing another one in a couple of hours. That is when the realization hit me. My mission is an adventure – to guard and protect, to let go and eventually set free. The latter is the hardest mission of all.

The Sign Of My Anxiety.

Broke

"You could die, you could die, or you could die." These are the three choices our physician recently gave my husband when asked what his alternatives were to checking himself into the hospital. Why any doctor would say this to a grown man is beyond me. Keith called me extremely upset, already in the emergency room, waiting for a bed. My 10-year-old handed me the phone saying it was a 911 issue with Dad. I immediately rushed to the ER, thankful that if this had to happen, it happened on the one day a week I have a babysitter at my house. She agreed to stay late, I called friends who agreed to take the kids overnight, and I was off, ready to face what was sure to be a grueling night, both mentally and physically.

Loads of emotions raced through me. My husband was told he could die. What would I do, a widow? How do I be strong and supportive for him in the ER when I wasn't sure how I was going to be strong and supportive for myself? Did I have enough life insurance? I know this sounds crass, but you'd be surprised what runs through your head on the way to an ER with a husband who was just handed that kind of information.

I found Keith on a gurney in the hallway of the ER. His area of the hallway even had a curtain he could pull for privacy. My only thought was, "if you are in the ER and something were to go wrong, I don't want that darn curtain in the way of anyone seeing it!" Needless to say, it remained open. The nurse attending us was a robust, friendly man. Humor was not something I expected to come so easily, but it did, to us all. Then the business lady came and had Keith sign away everything – we are insured, which explains the next exchange.

Right after signing these papers, the nurse hooked Keith up to a very potent antibiotic IV. Had he actually been waiting until the papers were signed before he administered it? I couldn't quite tell.

"How will this make me feel?" Keith asked, not knowing what to expect.

"Broke." The nurse replied, seriously this time. Keith thought he meant broken and hurt, shock registering on his face. I understood what he meant, immediately. "Poor," I said to Keith to quiet his quickly merging anxiety, and then I watched our entire family's Blue Cross 'Out of Pocket Maximum' drip into Keith's arm over the next two hours.

By the last drip, the Infectious Disease specialists and Ear Nose and Throat doctor on call arrived, together, fortuitously. Keith was still waiting for a bed in the hospital so the admittance procedure for an overnight (or longer) stay had not been finalized.

"This is not nearly as bad as we thought," both specialists agreed upon initial inspection of Keith's neck where the highly resistant MRSA Staph Infection has settled. It appeared subcutaneous – therefore not in his blood and not, at this point, life threatening. That was a huge relief.

"So, I won't have to stay in the hospital overnight?" Keith nearly pleaded. Neither of us wanted him to have to stay. "Well, you need the antibiotic drip," began the Infectious Disease doctor, a wonderfully knowledgeable man with, again, a good sense of humor. "There is a pill I could give you, but it's expensive," he continued. What kind of insurance do you have?"

"How expensive is it?" I could not believe we were in the middle of a financial health negotiation based on cash out vs. insurance, but I took it seriously, anyway.

"A lot. One hundred forty dollars a pill. He'll need two a day for two weeks. Blue Shield does not cover it. Blue Cross might."

Quickly calculating in my head, I knew that it would be cheaper to meet our $700 prescription deductible than it would to stay overnight in the hospital and meet that deductible. Even if Blue Cross didn't cover it, the $1,120 it would cost would be cheaper than the hospital stay. The last time a family member stayed over night, it was billed at more than six grand a night – just for the bed! That did not include any IV drips that make you feel 'broke' or anything else. And while we did not have to pay the full amount, we still had to meet our enormous $2500 per person deductible plus 30% of the negotiated rate over and above that.

The ENT turned out to be the father of two athletic and charming girls my boys have been in class with at their school. Again, he had a wonderful sense of humor and the banter was wonderful to help Keith take the edge off of realizing the position he was actually in. Together, the two doctors and a nurse cleaned out the affected area. Why I stood there to watch I'll never know. I can only liken it to a scene from "Alien" – and when I felt myself fainting, I just barely had the good sense to grab the nearest wall, squat down, and breathe deeply, slowly.

After Keith was all bandaged up, the ENT gave us his card and told Keith to come into his office the next Monday morning to have it redressed. The infectious disease doctor went over the pills and what to expect from the wound over the next several days. Oddly enough, both were leaving town within five days for vacation and wanted to make sure that Keith was well on his way to being healed before they left.

We thanked them profusely and smiled broadly when the robust male nurse came back surprised that Keith was not being admitted.

"It wasn't as bad as everyone thought," Keith said.

Still, it was bad enough to warrant a trip to the ER, to scare me and the kids and Keith himself to the point of reevaluation on what we all take for granted and the things we assume we'll have time to say and time to fix. And yes, bad enough to make us broke for the rest of the summer. Ah, well, at least we have each other.

Kids' (and Moms') Fitness Challenge

Out of necessity, over the winter break, I took both my boys to several of my outdoor exercise classes run by Eve Fleck of Gym Without Walls. Good old-fashioned physical fitness drills and cardiovascular training – rain or shine - on Friday mornings and Sunday mornings. They both moaned and groaned a bit, but finally decided it was better than staying at home and cleaning out their closets (which was the only alternative given to them). Several other moms brought their kids too.

After the initial, "It's too cold," "I don't want to this," etc... Kendall and Kamden and the other kids actually enjoyed it. Especially Kendall when he discovered he could beat me in sprints. What was interesting was seeing some of them get in touch with the competitive side of their personality. Kid vs. Mom. Kid vs. Kid. Mom vs. Everyone Else's Kids. It was fabulous fun.

It's because we brought our kids that Eve told us all about the Kids Fitness Challenge 5K at the Rose Bowl. My kids were instantly bugging me to register. All the Kids Fitness Challenge Events are free, so it was an easy decision. I logged on to www.fitnesschallengefoundation.org and pre-registered the three of us. The event is put on to encourage activity amongst school age children, awarding grants and equipment to the schools with the most participants on the day of the event. Out of the thousands of people there, we were the only representatives from our school, a fact that we will be trying to change having now experienced the event.

As our county's youth seems to be spiraling into a very unhealthful state of inactivity (regardless of how fervently they may shake that Wii remote), it was wonderful to see thousands and thousands of kids running and laughing like the young banshees that they are around the perimeter of the Rose Bowl. An impressive number of school buses filled the parking lots (this was a big event for several schools in attendance), event staff directed traffic, and police blocked off and barricaded the streets that we ran on.

Firefighters, corporate sponsors with booths and fabulous free give-a-ways, bouncy houses, climbing walls, the USC marching band, some local politicians and a few celebrities turned out to support the event through the Get Healthy California Expo and made it a wonderful and positive experience for all that attended. For me and for Kendall, one of the most exciting parts was being able to experience running out of the Rose Bowl tunnel into the end zone and actually being able to be on the grass level of the Rose Bowl field. We were fascinated at how beautiful the grass was – and that it was real. As someone who can barely get any grass to grow at all in my own backyard, I will definitely be looking into what type it is they use here that stands up to professional football.

This was our first 5K. It was a beautiful morning, with the sun shining and everything glistening from the hard rain the day before. But it was early (I can't remember the last time I saw a sunrise – LA is so beautiful at that time), it was cold, and the run seemed oddly longer than the 3.2 miles we knew it to be. But we had a great time, and ran most of it. Kendall actually sprinted the last leg – leaving me in the dust. We have already signed up for our second 5K in February – one in which there are actual prizes to be won, because while I just want to keep my kids moving and spend fun time with them, they want to feed their competitive natures and try to win something. What they don't realize yet is that by enjoying this experience and building a desire to do it again, they already have won.

Small Town Big City

Communities are no longer guaranteed by just moving into a neighborhood. I believe that you must create your own community. It is the people you surround yourself with and the people you choose to associate with that become a community for your family. My kids know who our community members are, the people other than their parents that they can turn to and trust.

And it is rare, I used to think impossible, to walk into a situation and find a whole new community of people to add to your existing one. But that is exactly the experience we had when we joined Sunrise Little League. Opening Day for Spring Baseball starts with a parade of floats. Having never participated in this before, we all reluctantly got up at 5 o'clock in the morning, Kamden got dressed in his Twins uniform, I made a large thermos of hot chocolate to share, we left the house while it was still dark, and we arrived at Woodlake Bowl by 6 a.m. I thought for sure we would be the first ones there at this unfriendly hour on a weekend morning, but we weren't.

I have never seen anything like it. The parking lot was full and bustling, large trucks creatively (and some appeared professionally) decorated with everything from team logos and mascots to baseball player cut outs to huge sound systems were all parked in the lot as parents and kids alike were busily adding the finishing touches to their team floats. Other kids, and most every kid there was in a baseball uniform, ran around full of glee.

The energy was infectious. I felt like a kid again myself and I grabbed a roll of streamers and started adding it to our team float. Some floats were very professional, others a bit more crafty, but all were glorious in their celebration of the children on the team that would get to ride on them. Around 7 am, police escorts arrived. Fire trucks arrived. And unless they were driving a float, all the parents got in their cars and headed toward Winnetka and Victory – to Sunrise Little League Park where the parade route ends.

It was hard for me to leave Kamden. But a wonderful woman I had known in nursery school and had just reconnected with because our boys were now on the same team, Christine Hardenberg, would be riding in the float along with the kids. I felt oddly safe leaving him in the back of a pick up truck with 17 other kids and a few adults that I barely knew. How cool to actually get to ride standing up in the back of the truck down Ventura Boulevard to Winnetka and Victory. Riding in the back of my dad's pickup truck used to be standard transportation in the 70's and 80's, but it never occurred to me that my kids would ever get that experience - what with all the safely guidelines and my being a huge safety advocate. So I kissed Kam and my husband, older son Kendall and I left to stake out a good spot to witness this remarkable parade. We found a great spot on Winnetka and parked the car. And where else do you sit for a parade but on the top of a mini van? We all climbed through the sunroof and anxiously awaited the first glimpse of the parade to come down the hill toward its final destination. Kendall was ecstatic to sit on top of the car. He waived at every passing automobile and acted as though he had won a small prize if they waived back.

And then the moment finally came - we were so excited! Everyone started cheering. Led by police escorts with sirens blaring to block traffic and keep the pace slow, the parade had reached the top of the hill on Winnetka to begin its decent toward Victory. It was truly magical. You could hear the music from the floats, hear the honking horns, and hear the squeals of delight from children of all ages on the floats. As each float passed us, we waved and hooted and cheered for everyone. Kendall saw kids he knew from school. He shouted at them, they shouted back. We saw Kamden's fall coach who called out from his float, "What team is Kam on?" Kendall, Keith and I shouted back from atop our van. "Twins!"

Everyone was smiling and cheering for everyone. Then Kam's float drove by. You could see the shock and delight on his face that we were on top of the minivan. He was standing up in the back of a pickup truck arms raised, fists pumping the air. He was having the time of his life. And so were we. After the last float, everyone merged into the first baseball diamond for a celebration of those that make this community possible, and for those that are moving on. It was very moving and as I looked around at all the people present, I was proud to be a part of it.

This was an experience that I will now look forward to every year. An experience that further defines and at the same time broadens my community. I feel so fortunate to live in the San Fernando Valley, the place that my kids, my family and I, call home.

No Car Needed Family Adventure Series Adventure #1 – Solana Beach

As gas prices once again soar, it becomes more and more difficult to just hop in the car to take the kids on an adventure. Just going to the mountains to throw a snowball becomes a costly adventure. Add in the whining the kids do in the car on the way up or the carsickness they get from staring down into their gameboys the entire drive and it's pretty much an altogether unpleasant experience. So my goal has become to create "No Car Needed Adventures." We will travel to somewhere new, without a car. We will explore new places on foot, without a car. We will rely on public transportation. My kids grumbled a bit at this suggestion, but I planned our first adventure anyway. A little 'outdoorsiness', exercise and fun exploring is good for everyone!

Trying to navigate the schedules of public transportation and coordinate them is a bit daunting at first. The Orange line. The bus lines. The Metro. Amtrak. Other trains. I began to wonder if I was perhaps biting off more than I could chew. So I scaled it back a bit and focused on a train adventure. My two boys have never been on a passenger rail train. Oddly, neither have I. So I searched online for stations near me. I settled on the Chatsworth Station – I can park my car there overnight and it is easy enough to get to. Then for stations around Southern California that we might want to go to – and preferably an area we are unfamiliar with to help with the need to adventure. We settled on Solana Beach. A beach town on HWY 101 in Southern California. I made reservations over the phone from information I gathered online. Tickets are cheaper if you make reservations 3 days in advance. And you can either pay on the train (Chatsworth is an unmanned station) or at the station itself, which I did for our return trip from Solana Beach. I booked a hotel – I again searched online then called the hotel directly (no cancellations fees that way). We packed one rolling bag for the 3 of us (that was the most challenging part of this adventure) – and away we went. We arrived at the station with time to spare. The kids were so excited about riding on a train. When the train finally arrived we boarded and took our seats. We were very lucky to get a booth- like seat with a table in-between so we could all sit and face each other. We talked. The train rocked and rolled side to side. The kids loved it. A very nice attendant named James served us snacks and beverages. The kids and I drew pictures at the table. My oldest read us stories from his book. We watched the scenery pass outside our train car as we traveled south. This was fabulous for me - to actually get to look around and notice things drivers don't have the luxury to notice. And to look into the faces of my children as we traveled. So far, worth every penny.

Three hours later we arrived in Solana Beach. Yes, the train ride is significantly longer than a car ride, but it was by far much more enjoyable. Hopping off the train we felt the exhilaration of being discombobulated. We had no idea where we were and no idea which direction to head in. So we held hands, my youngest insisted on rolling the luggage, the oldest on reading the MapQuest directions and map I had smartly printed to guide us from the train station to the hotel. And because I was not behind the wheel, and we had all the time in the world, I let him be in charge of it. He eventually guided us in the right direction and we took in the scenery, stores, landscaping, and occasional treasure found on the sidewalk during our walk to the hotel. I'm sure we were quite the sight - dragging luggage behind us as we walked. This was validated as we entered the hotel and the Customer Service Manager at the Courtyard Solana Beach greeted us behind the desk. As he said hello to my boys, I told him of our adventure, "Yes, I thought that was you I saw as I was driving in to work." He offered the boys fresh baked cookies – always present in the lobby and heavenly smelling – and gave us a lovely room. I asked if breakfast was included and he gave me a voucher for their restaurant. It's such a nice experience to talk to people about an adventure you're on – everyone seems to want to make it pleasant. We found our room on the second floor and boys do what they must – bounce from bed to bed. This to them signifies a true vacation – two big beds close enough to bounce to and fro from. We unpacked then ventured out. We took the opposite way we had come to our room from the lobby – exploring the hotel thoroughly is always part of an adventure. We eventually wound up outside the back of the hotel where we made our way about a block and a half down to the cliff where there was beach access. Solana Beach is a cliff beach town. There is no boardwalk, no beachfront homes or restaurants. There are beautiful condos and homes on the cliffs over looking the beach. And for most of the day, a large flat sandy beach with beautiful rocks and shells to collect for treasures. We made our way down the stairs. The sand was gorgeous - brown with ripples of black and full of what looked like fools gold. It truly shimmered in the afternoon light. We walked, collected rocks, watched the surfers and got our feet wet. Walking to the next set of stairs to take us back up the cliffs, we promised each other that first thing in the morning we would start here and continue our walk down the rest of the beach. Heading back to the hotel – the heated pool beckoned – we stopped at Pacific Grill to eat. A darling patio with good burgers, fries and chicken strips for the kids (and reasonable too, especially between 4 and 7pm where they have an extensive appetizer menu) made us all full and ready to continue on.

Suiting up, the kids jumped right in the pool. We had it all to ourselves. I sat in the gloriously bubbly Jacuzzi – now this is a vacation – and watched the kids play. After much pleading I joined them for pool style freeze tag. The pool was perfect adult temperature – even after a Jacuzzi – and very easy to get into – no chill at all. With daylight waning we quickly showered off, dressed and headed out, on foot, on a sidewalk further south. Within a few blocks of our hotel were the Del Mar Fairgrounds. Who knew?! We all made a note to definitely come back for horse races when the season opens. The beach across from the fairgrounds was small but lovely. Many dogs were playing in the ocean and on the beach. My kids were in heaven. They are so focused on dogs that I could not have planned this better even if I tried. They reveled in the dogs being all around them and begged to bring our dog here one day. As the sunset over the ocean turned the few fluffy clouds in the sky pink, we headed back to the hotel. We bought some microwave popcorn in the lobby. All rooms are equipped with microwave, mini fridge, and mini coffee maker. We ate, talked about our plan for the next day and fell into a deep slumber, as we were all exhausted.

I'd like to personally thank the inventor of black out curtains – my kids slept and slept and slept. I actually had to wake them up. This truly is a vacation! The smell of bacon and syrup wafting up to our room from the courtyard restaurant was more than I could bear. Finally, my little sleepy heads rose from their slumber and we headed out. A delicious buffet of hot and cold breakfast foods satiated us. The kids kept going back for more – when else can you get fresh made waffles, French toast, cereal, eggs, sausage, bacon, fruit, yogurt, muffins, bagels, juice and hot cocoa all at the same breakfast except on vacation? That they were able to walk out of there was a minor miracle. The fresh ocean breeze reinvigorated them and we walked down the street behind the hotel to the last set of stairs we had come up yesterday.

As we headed down, we encountered and older man in wetsuit with a huge fish on a rope. The kids were mesmerized by it. It was a huge halibut that he had just caught. Is that legal? I thought to myself, not wanting to spoil the moment for my kids. Then I heard them laugh. Half way down the steps you could see what was just yesterday a large sandy beach, and what this morning was nothing but waves coming all the way up to the cliffs. We stood and watched in wonderment. Wow. How would we continue on our adventure without a boat? The tide seemed to be going out as the waves were not coming up as high and you could finally see a stretch of sand. As soon as it seemed plausible we continued down the steps and onto the beach. Our final destination was to be Fletchers Cove, the most famous of beaches in Solana Beach.

So we jumped in, literally, jumped into the water and dashed as quickly as we could before another wave came. In retrospect this was not the safest thing to do. Even though the boys were squealing with delight as we all got soaked, I was holding on to their arms very tightly so as not to allow them to be washed away by the next wave. Running in between waves became the only way to get back to dry land. It was too wet to turn back. We finally made it to our destination, where the boys immediately started digging in the sand. Other beachgoers were in their bathing suits. We looked like quite the tourists in our wet sweats and shoes. Squishing uncomfortably up the hills and along the streets back to our hotel, we snuck in the back, rinsed off and dropped all our clothes in the washing machine. Thank god for laundry facilities! We packed up, and headed out, luggage in tow, stopping along the way at all the great little shops on the other side of the railroad tracks. We slowly made our way to the train station, where we reluctantly, but happily boarded for our journey home. Luckily, we were able to get the same seats we had on the ride down. This time, we enjoyed the different light outside on the ocean and the hills as they passed – for it was nearing sunset as we returned home. It amazes me that we don't talk about these things more often. But in that moment, that was all we had to focus on – our surroundings and each other. And that was a journey in and of itself. We are already planning our next one.

Playing on Solana beach during our first No Car Needed Adventure.

Catalina? Yes! Another No Car Needed Adventure

I nearly fainted when I received my Amex bill from our car trip to Carmel (a.k.a. "Bathroom Mission Adventure"). The amount of money I spent on gas was daunting. So when my boys wanted to have an adventure day over spring break, we discussed many options and finally settled on Catalina. It's close. They've never been. They had not yet experienced a boat trip and were thus very excited by the prospect. I could also do the trip in one day (saving on hotel costs), and I could do it without a car! I figure if I am going to plunk down that kind of money for transportation, it might as well be on something that gets us around in a different manner. And to top it all off, my husband, Keith, would actually be able to join us on this one-day excursion.

We bought our Catalina Express tickets online a few days before our adventure day. This ensured us a seat on what was sure to be a packed vessel. Arriving in San Pedro with about 45 minutes to spare, we collected our tickets and wandered around the port. The kids were in awe of the massive cranes taking the cargo on and off giant ships. Inside the port we looked over the pamphlets of touristy things to do on Catalina and settled on a "submarine" tour of the protected cove. There are many things to do on the island, so we picked a few and bought tickets for just this one, leaving us some flexibility for the rest of our day.

Boarding the ship, Kendall was determined to sit on the top open level. It was foggy and cold, so Kamden and I headed to the protected seats inside the boat while Kendall and Keith scoped out seats above. The plan was that we could all switch, but that we would have two seats in each area saved as the boat was indeed fully booked. It's nice having another adult on our adventures to expand our options. As we left the bay, Kamden couldn't contain himself. "I love being on a boat! This is the best ever! Thank you, Mom!" Wow. All that and our adventure had just started. The sea was rough and waves splashed at the windows. Kendall and Kamden wandered up and down between the upper deck and enclosed seats below. I tried to wander, but alas, was struck with horrible seasickness. There is a reason I don't understand the boat life. Thank goodness Keith was with us. He has much better sea legs, so he wandered with the boys as I sat with my head down, plastic bag at the ready.

Finally docking after an hour at sea, we disembarked and I immediately felt better. The kids took off - running to all the tourist booths looking for what we might get into. Parasailing (too cold). Bikes – even tandem ones (too much work, the island is very hilly). Golf Carts – now there is a definite possibility. Glass bottom boat tours – we already had the submarine tour booked. Kayaks - again, too cold. Speed boats – see Kayaks and Parasailing. There was actually a lot more to do when you have your kids in mind than I remember as just an adult get-a-way spot.

We grabbed a delicious lunch at Armstrong's Seafood Restaurant. Sitting on their outside deck with the lapping water visible through the cracks in the wooden deck, we truly felt like we were far away from home. At lunch, I noticed that Keith was not quite in the spirit of our adventure day, for he kept saying the word, "No." "Keith," I said sweetly, "we are on an adventure, can you please try to say the word, 'Yes' instead of, 'No'?" He looked a bit shocked, paused, smiled and smartly said, "Yes!" I asked him if his food was good, "Yes," he replied. "Will you buy me another hat?" "Yes!" Then the kids got in on our game, "Can we have dessert even though we just had soda?" they asked. "Yes," their dad replied. Now we were all giggling, I even snorted, for we knew this would go on the whole day.

We wandered through town and through all the great shops, the kids scoping out what they might want to take home as a souvenir. I found several fabulous hats to buy. Have I mentioned I am a hat person? The kids finally settled on prehistoric sharks teeth from the Catalina Island Conservancy. "Can we buy this?" And because they had scoped out several stores and made a decision, Keith gladly said, although slowly for effect, "Yes."

Our undersea, semi-submersible tour on the Discovery Tours "Starlight" vessel was amazing. We all truly felt as though we were boarding a submarine, but thankfully it was large and airy on the inside with lots of vented cool air blowing hard so that even the slightest bit of my claustrophobia would be abated. That and the very funny young tour guide immediately announced that we were not trapped below - we could go up on the deck at any time. The big windows in front of each seat give a wonderful view of the sea below. It's like scuba diving without getting wet. Fish come right up to the windows, and the kelp forests below sway in rhythm with the ocean and are magnificent. The bright orange fish, the Garibaldi, which is the California state marine fish (who knew), and is protected, shone brightly and proudly amongst the blues and greens of the sea. The 45-minute tour was much too short, leaving us all wanting to explore this new world even more.

Upon disembarking from our sub, we all decided the next best thing would be a golf cart tour of the island. We rented our cart from Island Rentals, a hospitable and kindly group who reminded us that all carts must be returned before 6pm. Had we known that, we might have done this first. Still, we all hopped in, the kids of course fighting over shotgun, and took off. Or should I say puttered off. The carts move at a steady pace between 10 to 15 miles per hour - regardless of whether you are on flat, uphill or downhill terrain. At one point, Kendall stated that he was certain he could out run us. "Prove it," I said. Out he went onto the sidewalk. "On your mark, get set, go!" and we were off, Kendall trying his hardest to outrun us and Keith, Kamden and I laughing hysterically in the cart. Even though we puttered along, we were still able to beat Kendall. "My turn!" I got out of the car and on "Go" began a slow motion rendition of what can only be likened to a hobbled runner. Keith immediately caught on and pretended to make the cart go as fast as it could. The kids screamed in protest, as even though I picked up my slow motion pace, they knew we were cheating and that I would indeed beat the cart - which annoyed Kendall to no end. In the end we were all laughing so hard we had to stop to take a breath.

Up and down the hills we went. Pointing out the odds and ends, new construction, beautiful breathtaking views, and the carts that were actually going slower than ours. Not to be outdone, Keith was certain he could actually out run us and hopped out. He was ahead for a bit as he had the element of surprise on his side, but our putt cart eventually overtook him -

and ditched him. Ha! He eventually caught up after we swung back around to get him. The rest of the ride was spent inside the cart laughing and enjoying one another and the fresh Catalina air. Silliness and laughter are wonderful ways to bond with your family.

After an hour we had made all the rounds on the map and returned our cart to the cart shack. We decided to have dinner at one of the restaurants we had passed along the way. After a good meal (where we were witness to the most somber and odd wedding party you have ever seen), we headed back for the boat, for it was very close to our departure time. Running through town I am sure we were quite the sight, laughing, giggling, and dodging each other in a raucous game of tag. Somehow, I always wind up "it."

"Okay, that's not our boat," explained Kamden as we stood in line to get onto the last departing Catalina Express. Indeed, this was a much bigger version of what we had taken over, but we checked with the attendant and we were definitely in the right line. This boat was at least two times bigger. We grabbed what seats were left – sadly no window seats, and all decided to stay below deck as it was now very cold outside. We recounted the fun of the day and marveled at how much smoother and faster this boat was than the previous one. Note to self: next time, make sure to request only this size boat. Not an ounce of seasickness.

"Can I have a hot chocolate?" "Yes," I said. The boys drank it down. Then later, "Can I have a candy?" "No," Keith said. All faces fell. Alas, the end to another adventure day had come. We disembarked and marveled at how glorious the San Pedro docks look when lit up at night. As we reluctantly made our way back to the regular transportation that would take us home, the kids were very chatty.

"What kind of transportation will we take for our next No Car Needed Adventure? A helicopter?" Kendall said hopefully. "We'll think of something, I'm sure," I replied.

"It feels like we were gone a lot longer than a day. This was a great, great day! Thanks Mom." And that comment from Kamden will make me smile when my next Amex bill arrives. It was worth every penny.

Elvis Renewed Our Love

Elvis lives. And he remarried me and my husband in Las Vegas last Friday.

After ten years, two kids and our share of ups and downs, we wanted and needed to do something special for our tenth anniversary. We joked about Elvis marrying us the first time, but opted instead for the big fancy wedding. We did, however, promise that Elvis would be our big 10-year gift to us and whoosh! the ten years have blown by. So I knew that Elvis would renew our love. Nothing big. Nothing fancy. Just me, my husband, our two kids, Elvis and Vegas, baby.

So I booked the hotel - the Paris in Las Vegas (it's thematic as my husband proposed on the real Eiffel Tower in France) and booked the Elvis Chapel through vivalasvegas.com. The afternoon before we were scheduled to leave, I rushed around with my sister in law and my two boys in tow, bought a gown on clearance, dug up an old costume tiara - every girl should wear a tiara any chance she gets - fashioned a veil out of a bolt of tulle from my closet, ran out again to purchase fake flowers for my bouquet and boutonnieres, then raced back home and packed up. It is exhausting planning a wedding and outfitting everyone for it in one day.

Maybe it's me, but you forget how brown the drive to Vegas is. On the roadway an oddly large number of cars painted with blazing advertisements for 'traveling manicurists' passed us. The one thing I forgot to do. My nails.

Pulling into town, we couldn't help but smile and feel giddy with the anticipation of all the possibilities Vegas presents. So many new hotels! Such fabulous theming! The kids were pointing and yelling out both sides of the car window, "Look it's New York! Look at the fire on that Giant Screen TV! Look it's the Eiffel Tower! Look at her naked bum!" I stammered something about appropriateness, unable to come up with a real response to their excitement over all the naked female body parts.

We pulled into the Paris Hotel and ran in to explore all the sights. My eight-year-old thought he had gone to heaven. "A huge arcade!" he exclaimed. I sadly had to walk him off the gambling floor and explain that this version of heaven is only for those twenty-one and over. He said nothing, but I could see the math working in his little head. He gazed around the giant and noisy room. Only thirteen more years. He happily settled for bouncing on the beds with his brother. And swimming in the pool, until it was decided that not even they could swim in such cigarette, cigar and trash infested water. This hotel definitely does not cater to the family crowd.

On Friday afternoon we all got dressed in our wedding 'costumes' - it felt like we were playing dress up. Me in my gown, tiara and veil. My husband and kids in suits complete with boutonnieres. Walking through the hotel with people smiling, staring and saying, "Congratulations!" I felt for a brief time like a blushing bride again. My favorite moments were the few little girls we passed along the way - they were in awe of the tiara, the flowing gown and veil. Their expressions and gasps of little girl dreams made me feel like a real princess and suddenly I had the urge to apply for a job as Cinderella at Disneyland. The imagination of a child really can make your dream come true.

Outside the hotel our limousine awaited. There is nothing like breezing through the crowds to a driver standing with the door open to a stretch limousine to make you feel like royalty. Upon arrival at the chapel we did a quick rehearsal then got right to the ceremony. Elvis looked quite swanky in his deep cut jewel encrusted white suit that hugged his tight young body. (Oops! Put those thoughts aside, girl, you are getting married!) I walked down the aisle, escorted by my beautiful boys, to Elvis singing in a fabulous voice "I can't help falling in love". My husband waited next to Elvis. We all danced while Elvis sang. We waved to the internet cam mounted above Elvis and hoped that some of our friends and family around the globe had received our e-vite in time and had logged on to watch and share this fabulous moment with us. We danced with our kids, promised not to get our blue suede shoes wet, darted around the "obey" part of the ceremony, took some photos with Elvis and that was that! As we burst out of the chapel doors to an awaiting audience of one (the photographer) our names shone brightly on the huge chapel marquee. As we all smiled at the camera, Elvis by our side, all I could think was, "Thank God my Christmas card photo for this year is done!"

Upon request, Elvis signed my virginal white garter, compliments of the package we had purchased, and then waved goodbye as we glided back into the limousine. We were giddy from our fun experience. The kids were beaming from ear to ear. And I was glad that we had taken the time to create a memory. To strengthen a bond. The marriage bond. The family bond. The bond of love, laughter and adventure.

Take A Stand

As our society becomes overwhelmed with excessive consumerism and lack of values, it becomes hard to discern a true table scrap from what should be thrown to the dogs.

But that does not mean you should stop considering each and every piece as you come across it.

Please do. Do consider each piece. Don't just toss it all out of habit.

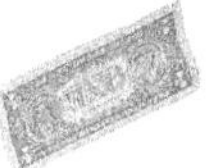

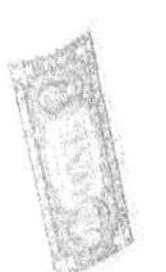

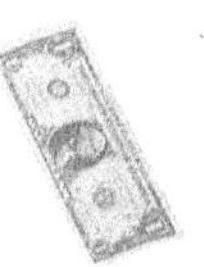

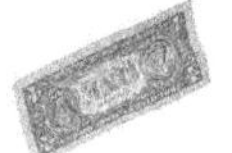

Who Are Your Neighbors?

Driving home after picking my kids up from school I noticed a familiar car on the side of the road. It's an odd shaped car, which is why I recognized it. The hood was up and a gas can lay to the side of it in the grass. "Isn't that our neighbor?" I asked the kids. "Yes! We should stop and help," they answered eagerly. It was, of course, the right thing to do. I pulled my car up slowly and a man came around from behind the car. "Do you live around the corner and up the street?" I asked. "Yes," he replied, obviously wondering why a woman with two kids in a minivan would stop and ask. "I live two houses up from yours, do you need help?" As it turns out he was in the process of fixing the problem, but thanked me for stopping.

What struck my boys and me on our short drive home was that we had recognized the car, not the person. This man and his wife live two houses down from us and we have never met him. I've met the wife, she seems lovely and personable from the few conversations we've had in the nine years we have been neighbors, but the husband (a relatively new addition to the neighborhood) has lived there for at least two years and not one of us recognized him. Just the car. This made me question what kind of community and neighborhood I had created for my children. Why didn't we know these people? Why don't they know us? Why don't we know our neighbors? Isn't a wonderful neighborhood part of the American Dream?

My youngest son, Kamden, is in the second grade at Wilbur Avenue Elementary School. A highlight of this year has been a unit that his teacher,

Mrs. Stein, has her class participate in every year, a unit called "The Ancestor Fair." For this project, each child researches an ancestor, writes a state or country report about where he/she was born, creates an oral presentation in the first person about the life of the ancestor, makes a paper doll decorated to look like this person, and finally "becomes" them by dressing as the ancestor and bringing artifacts/souvenirs about them as well as providing a sampling of their favorite food to share with each person that attends the fair. During this project, the children discover amazing information about one another, as much of the work is done in class. They all learn where each child's family is from – over 13 countries were represented this year, as well as the various family religions – from Catholicism to Judaism to Islam. They experience through each other the hardships and triumphs of each family – from losing children crossing America in a covered wagon to the successful rescue of a captured Iranian Army General. They explore the cultural traditions and fashions of each family – from a glamorous New York Jewish woman to a multilingual and musical Renaissance man from France. Finally, the various foods brought in represent all the differences mentioned above and play a big part in the Ancestor Fair - food that I would never think of exposing my seven year old to, but that has now widened our world and become part of our culinary repertoire. Who knew stuffed cabbage, empanadas and lefse tasted so good?

The most wonderful aspect of the Ancestor Fair is that the kids are truly interested in and fascinated to learn about the differences of each of their classmates. Fascinated and accepting. There is no judgment, only celebration and a willingness to want to try new things for themselves. No preconceived notions of what is normal or acceptable – it is all normal, all acceptable. No color lines. No religious lines. No social lines. Just an awe at how different they all can be, yet how similar at the same time. Mrs. Stein has created for these kids, for my kid, a microcosm of what our world should be like. She has shown them how to delight in finding out about the neighbors in their little community – neighbors that are perhaps just one or two desks over or maybe all the way across the room, but they are all neighbors nonetheless.

What do you know about your neighbors? Where are they from? What do they believe? What is their favorite food? Personally, I barely talk to my neighbors. I chalk it up to the fact that I am always shuttling kids to and from somewhere and that everyone is just too busy. But my neighborhood is changing. A new family is moving in four houses away from mine. Their kids are younger than mine, but still, my own children are very excited about the fact that there will be more kids around. I feel like this is an opportunity for the whole street, for our neighborhood to get to know one another. Our little community is changing, so I am going to seize this chance to get to know my neighbors better. To be able to recognize them, not just their cars. To find out about their worlds, their past and their present.

Just because we all live behind different doors, we do actually all live in the same neighborhood, in the same community, and regardless of our beliefs, our color, our social status or our favorite food, we all basically want the same things. The same things we wanted in second grade. We all want to have friends. We all want to make connections with other people. We all want to feel safe. We all want to know that we are part of something larger – just like our ancestors before us. Ancestors who were once again brought to life by Mrs. Stein's second grade class to teach us all a little something about ourselves, our communities, our neighborhoods – big and small – today, tomorrow, around the world.

Win, Lose, or Blame?

This is directed at the parent who yelled at the referee during the soccer game. The parent who sauntered across the field, yelling, "You will pay!" at the ten, eleven and twelve year-old boys. The parent who started yelling at the coach and parents of the opposite team.

This is directed at the coach who allowed a parent on his team to get away with that behavior, stopping the game, and forcing our children to have to witness such appalling behavior.

This is to the coach who threw his clipboard, who in earshot of the opposing team, told the kids on his team that they lost only because the referee made bad calls. That they should have won the game, "if not for the referee."

This is for the parent who walks up and down the line screaming inappropriately at your kid and every kid, thinking that what he has to offer obviously out ranks that of the coaches.

To all these parents, I'd like to let you in on a secret: YOU ARE AN EMBARRASSMENT. Your kids are mortified – they do not think your behavior is cool. The parents around you – at least those who chose not to participate in your tantrum - are horrified. And most of all, you are doing your young athlete, your kid, a huge disservice.

In these games, as in life, there will be a winner and a loser. And as a microcosm for our world, in these games, as parents it is up to us to teach our children how to cope. No, it is not always fair. Sometimes, the better team, the better player, will lose. But that is reality. Should you blame someone? Why? It is what it is. It is the ref's job to call the game. Whether he does it to your liking is not really the point. It is his job, not yours. And the kids have to deal with it.

Telling your kids they lost because of bad weather, rotten field conditions, erroneous calls by the ref or because it just wasn't their day teaches them NOTHING. Let them learn to fail. Let them learn that sometimes the calls will not be in their favor. Let them learn to accept it and PLAY ON.

I grew up a competitive athlete, and one of my best friends' mothers would rip her apart after a meet if she didn't break her own records. It was embarrassing for me to witness and so demoralizing to my friend that she never talked about it. The mother, of course, thought she was inspiring her young athlete to the next level. Truthfully she was just shaming her.

As a parent now of two young athletes, I do cheer on the sidelines. I get involved and sometimes the games are very exciting and tense. Sometimes certain calls/coaching decisions/players irk me – on my team and the opposing team. But I cheer on. Not blame on. Not tantrum on. Not give excuses for what went on.

Our kids need to learn that there are winners and losers. And that they may/will be on both sides. And yes, sometimes it will be due to bad calls/ field conditions/coaching/refereeing - but ultimately, it JUST IS WHAT IT IS. Win with grace. Lose with grace. Let them learn the art of good sportsmanship. Let them learn to persevere, learn from it and grow from it. Let them learn that this is what life is like. And let them learn that you will cheer for them and love them WIN or LOSE.

Yours and Mine

Standing in line behind a cute kid (your child?) at the ice-cream truck, my two boys and I watched as he bought a BB gun. He was so excited! The rectangular factory shrink-wrapped box depicted a picture of the promise inside. "It looks soooo real!" he exclaimed to his friends as they high-fived each other. My kids took in this new information – you can buy guns from the ice-cream man?

"May I see that?" I asked him. Silence. Stares from him and his friends. And from the ice-cream man. A respectful young man, he handed me his purchase. I stared at it in horror. It was a 6mm air powered BB gun clearly marked, "Not a toy. Adult supervision required." I showed him that this was not a play gun, that this was a real and dangerous weapon. He looked at me and managed an "I had no idea." " I know," I said.

All attention turned to the ice-cream man – an adult preying on the naiveté and trust of our elementary school children. "This is clearly not a toy!" I said. I helped the boy return the gun and get his money back. He seemed relieved. He smiled and waved as he wandered away with his friends finding a renewed excitement in something else. He was only 8 or 9 years old after all.

Standing there, watching the group walk away, I felt a tug on my leg. "Mom, what about us? Can we buy a toy too with our ice-cream?" I smiled at my kids, handing them each two dollars to make their choices – supervised choices because children lack the ability to always make wise decisions for themselves. Especially when it does not occur to them that the decision could be harmful. That's what they count on adults for. And yes, some adults like the ice-cream man hawking guns will let them down, but you and I will not. For we all need to guard each other's children from time to time. I will do it for your child. I hope you will do the same for mine.

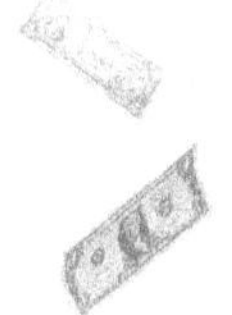

Brohawk Litmus Test

By definition (and yes, I had to look it up), a litmus test is "a test in which a single factor (such as an attitude) is decisive." Now, I like to think I am a non-judgmental, progressive person. I live in a city where neighbors are not of the same race, religion or social background, a melting pot of tolerance and acceptance. Or so I thought. At least until my two young boys wanted mohawks for the summer. They begged during school and at some point I must have said they could get one over the summer. I forgot about it. They did not. So off we went to Fantastic Sam's and off came their hair – all but a longish row down the center of their head that stood on end, full of hair glue. They are sweet, smart, sensitive boys. And shaving hair off the sides of their head does not shave off who they are on the inside. Again, or so I thought. Thus began this litmus test.

Right after the haircuts, we ran errands. A man with daughters slightly older than my kids rudely commented on my children's new hair. Loudly. In the middle of the grocery store. Instantly, my "mama bear" instinct rose up to block this verbal intruder ready to roar at him or his kids about the way they looked. But I didn't, for that is not who I am or who I want my kids to be. And while my kids didn't hear him, I was very shaken up. I had not prepared myself for that kind of reaction. In my own neighborhood! He did not notice how cute or how well behaved they were in the grocery store. He only thought they were trouble-making kids with bad attitudes. Because of their hair. I tried to ignore it, but now I feared my kids were vulnerable thus testing my tolerance of their desire to experiment outside the "everyone is the same" mentality. Later, we went out to eat and the teenagers at the restaurant loved the two young brothers with mohawks, dubbing them "Brohawks". At least they were cool in the teenage crowd.

The next day a friend picked them up for a playdate. She was speechless (a rarity for her). When she did speak, my face stung as though she had slapped me. "What happened to the nice young boys I adore?" She blurted out in front of my kids! As though a hair cut redefines them as a person! Her view of who they are as human beings changed in that moment. "They are still the same kids!" I retorted, a little too loudly. "It's just hair!" As they climbed into her car, I sadly and for the first time nervously wondered, "would she treat them differently in her home?" I anxiously fumed the whole time. This woman was married to a professional rock musician. Her own son has long hair. I flashed to my high school experience where the long hair rockers and mohawk punkers disliked each other. Will the rockers and punkers be friends in this next generation? Not if today is an example of the parental attitudes being passed on to six and eight year olds.

As the summer wore on, we started to see more kids with mohawks. The acceptance level increased. A few adults looked on in dismay, but as it was now a fad, the harsh judgments ceased.

As a parent I strive to teach my kids what is right and wrong. To be good, respectful, sensitive people. Regardless of what their friends are doing. But breaking from the norm and exploring their own desires with something as safe as hair put them at risk for being ostracized. And oddly, not by the kids. It was the parents who came down harsh on their new look. The parents who spoke intolerance. And if kids reflect their parents' behavior, then a new generation of intolerance is born. So let us as parents determine what deserves intolerance. Drugs. Destructive Behavior. Racism. Not hair cuts on kids. Not kids experimenting with their individuality and creativity. Let's not allow our old biases to get in the way of what we teach our children today.

Kamden and Kendall sport the Brohawk look.

They are the sweetest boys ever!

Manners, Civility, and Charm, Oh My!

Manners. Responsibility. Respect. These are attributes that are important to me, and I believe, to our society. Attributes that I am parenting my children to accomplish. Attributes that I demand from others, even children. Attributes that hopefully you will demand from my kids and me (and that I hope we live up to).

Recently, I experienced a flash back into my own past as I received in the mail an invitation for my fifth grade son to attend the Valley Cotillion. Immediately, the pink dress and white gloves I wore to Cotillion in middle school flashed through my mind. I had not thought about Cotillion since I attended in the seventh and eighth grades.

For one reason or another, it did not even occur to me to look into it for my children. I suppose I figured it had fallen by the wayside. After all, who talks about sending their children to charm school anymore?

Cotillion, if you have never heard of it before, is a series of six semi-formal parties where etiquette instruction, good manners, social skills, graces, and self confidence are taught to boys and girls in order to prepare them to handle any social situation with grace. The dress is semi-formal: dresses, gloves, heels for the girls; suits, ties, dress shoes for the boys.

Kendall in a five piece suit learning how to appropriately behave in a formal setting, dance with a girl, carry on a conversation with a girl or (gasp!) her parents, and knowing which fork to use? I signed him up immediately. I excitedly shared this little rediscovery with other moms, and Kendall wound up with his best buddies from school attending Cotillion with him.

The boys, Nick Bodnar and Julian Gordy are in fifth grade with Kendall and all were a bit reluctant at first. I tried not to talk about it much so as not to get any flack from Kendall at home, but when I received the five piece suit I had ordered in the mail I ripped it open and showed him what he would be wearing.

"Cool," Kendall said, inspecting the tie, vest, blazer, white shirt and dress slacks. "What shoes will I wear?" I couldn't have hoped for a better reaction.

The night of the first party, we all congregated at the Gordy residence. MB, Julian's dad, was the only husband available that day to help the boys tie a tie. Lesson number one. Check. Kendall actually chose to wear a decorative handkerchief as well, something his friends immediately envied. They are all developing their own style and this was yet another way for them to express it – tie, handkerchief, and next party? A flower, for sure.

MB took the boys to the event while I, Cindy and Trish (the moms), though disappointed, headed off to back to school night where we proudly shared photos on our cameras of our little men.

"What is Cotillion and how do I sign my kid up," we heard this over and over. We had rediscovered a treasure.

"That was great! We learned how to properly walk a lady around. Here, let me show you." Kendall showed me in our kitchen when he got home that night. "And we learned three dances – the Waltz, the Patty Cake and another one. Let me show you." He waltzed me around upstairs as I was trying to get him to bed. But he was too excited to sleep. "All the girls wore gloves, and to have a snack, they must take them off finger by finger. And I am supposed to let you lead the conversation." Once again, he demonstrated his newly acquired knowledge. Somehow I don't think one-word answers, with me asking all the questions are what the instructors had in mind, but he is eager to go back and learn more. And that is a charming gift in and of itself.

It's A Chore

"Your kids do what?" This was the incredulous question I received from several women with whom I was discussing what our kids do (or don't do) to help around the house.

"How much do you pay them?" One asked. I felt the need to remind them that no one pays me do housework, but I didn't.

"They don't get an allowance at this point. They get the privilege of living in their home and being part of the family," I stated, feeling as though I had indeed done a good job in the motherhood department. But I was met with an odd silence. It was awkward. What were they thinking? I had to break it. "Don't your kids do chores?" Heads started shaking. "No."

Let me preface this exchange by stating that I am a neat and tidy person, but not a fanatic. I need order to function. I also need things to be clean (I could blame it on allergies or sinuses, but then I would be such a cliché). The flat truth is, I do not live in my house alone. I do not make a lot of the mess. I have two able bodied sons who need to be raised in such a way that my future daughters-in-law will love me and thank me. Why shouldn't they be washing down the hand-printed walls and mopping the muddy floors? There is no reason. They should. And they have been - pretty much since they could toddle about. Of course, back then it was a game. Now, they know it's just a chore.

But, because I demand their help for the chores, I do try to make it fun (they are still kids after all). Have you seen the cool micro fiber hand mitts you and your kids can wear to dust and clean? And the best thing about them is they don't need any harsh cleaning products – the dust and crud stick right to them. Same for the micro fiber floor dusters that have replaced my broom. I never knew how much dust we all kicked back up to the chairs and tables and cabinets just by sweeping. And the Mr. Clean Magic Eraser is just that – magical. It truly takes off pretty much anything. It even took off sharpie from my kid's white headboard. And it is shaped like a big eraser so the kids love it. Don't you remember how you adored your collection of erasers in elementary school? This makes a fine addition.

I'm not fooling myself, my kids don't love chores. But they do them. Some they like more than others. "I like to skate mop," says Kendall. Skate mopping is where you put hot wet rags under your feet and, yep, skate around the floors. "But I don't like weeding." "Neither do I," chimed in Kamden, "but I do like planting." "That's because he likes giving things life, not killing things," Kendall observed about his little brother during this exchange. Wow. All of a sudden, this felt like a deepening conversation. He gleaned this from what his brother does and doesn't like about chores? "What about me?" I asked. He paused. "You just like things clean." Nothing deep about that.

These household duties are good for my boys. They each have a list, they know what is expected and they take their responsibilities seriously (because if they didn't the Wii disappears). "I feel like I accomplished something and I feel good about myself," Kamden tells me when asked what he likes about his chores. "Really?" I try to keep this line of communication going. "Yeah, I like it best when we are all doing them together – that makes it fun." Who knew - cleaning time and chore time can be good quality family time. Now that's time well spent.

Political Futures

I received a phone call confirming my reservation for Senator Hillary Clinton's Town Hall Meeting at 2:15pm in the Grand Salon at CSUN. I explained to the young female voice on the other end that I was pulling my eleven year-old son out of school and wanted to make sure we got in. She told me that if I got there an hour early we'd be fine. We weren't. Pulling into the parking lot at 12:45, sipping on our drive through drinks, we could see a line of people snaking down a very long path.

I hurriedly bought a parking pass, which probably put us at least another twenty people back as I was the only one bothering to do so, and hustled into the line. It was cold and the wind was biting. I questioned the people in line to make sure that we were indeed in the right place.

"How many people are in front of us?" Kendall asked. No one around us seemed to know. I stood in line and watched him as he walked, and walked, and walked, nearly out of sight to the front and back. At least three hundred he guessed. Disappointed, I decided to walk up as well, assuring those in line around me that if they saved our spots I would try to get us all some information. The woman working the front of the line was not hopeful that we would get in, regardless of the fact I had made a reservation or been told that getting there by 1 pm was fine, regardless of the fact that I had pulled my son out of school. Still, Kendall wanted to stay. We became friendly with our fellow line members. The two women in front of us worked at the University and were very lively and adamant Hillary supporters. The gentleman wearing an expensively cut business suit behind us was a supporter as well.

I am a registered Republican. Which doesn't mean much, really, because I am all about the conversation, the discussion. And now so is my kid. Who, by the way, was the only child there that we could see, in what grew to be a line of nearly a thousand people.

Prior to signing up for this event, I had a group of women and their kids over to my house. As the kids ran around, we sat and discussed the candidates, the issues and what it all meant to us. Surprisingly, everyone had differing opinions on what was actually going on. Some were better versed than others, some were just party loyalists, but all felt strongly regardless and the kids found this fascinating.

I relish the conversation. Talk to me. Tell me why I should think the way you think. Let's have a point, counterpoint repartee. It challenges the thought process and the reasoning behind it. And the discoveries - if only about the other person - fascinate me. Unfortunately, I don't find many people who love it the way I do. But these discussions have changed minds, or at least were the impetus to get people to think about things differently.

Which is why when Senator Hillary Clinton came to town to speak, I reserved seats for two. For my son, Kendall, and me. He is the future after all. And this election will influence his future. Which is why I want him to be a part of the discussion now. He is in student government at his school because he likes to have an opinion and likes to talk with those people who have opinions too. He is also fiercely competitive. And unless you know what you are talking about, it is hard to compete in politics.

We did not get in to that Town Hall Meeting. But I would like to take my kids to another one. And they would like to attend one. As would many other kids and parents I know. So, Senators Clinton, Obama, McCain; former Senator Edwards; and governors Romney and Huckabee, I will continue to listen to you and have conversation about you and I'd be happy to host a small town meeting at my house if you'd come meet with those who have not made up their minds, who are still having the discussions, and whose children are an actual influence on the conversations we are having, and the votes we will be placing.

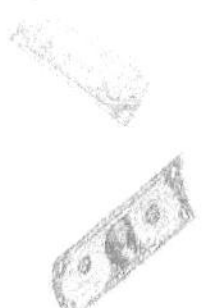

Who do you think you are?

That's it. We live in a world of too much permission. Who do you think you are? You think you can call anyone and start yelling at him or her not having been part of the issue and not knowing what went on? You think you can say you don't care if they are treated badly and that it will be all right with the person you are talking to? You think it is all right if others suffer as long as you get your way? You think you can park your car anywhere you want? You think you can say anything to anyone and do anything to anyone without consequence? Yes, evidently you do. You have proven it on many occasions. And sadly, it has become clear it is our society's fault you behave this way. Our fault because we let you get away with it. Our fault because we do not say anything to enforce the rules of our society. Our fault because we do not demand you show respect for other human beings. You only demand people show it to you.

Well, our society will no longer tolerate you and your childish self-centered outlook. It will no longer be my fault. How dare you set such a poor example for the children that you are around – at home, on the soccer field, at the mall, in a restaurant. How dare you set such a poor example for the staff that runs your business for you. How dare you set such a poor example of what it means to be a positive contributor to our society. Shame on you for behaving that way. Shame on us for letting you get by with it for so long.

Why do we let you get by with it? Because you are loud and abrasive and we don't want to cross paths with you? Because you are the boss of someone? Because you have a lot of money? Because we are afraid you may attack us or sue us if we step up to you? Shame on us for perpetuating your reality. Shame on us for not taking the good of our society as a whole into consideration when we let you get by with just one more self-centered adolescent behavior. You are an adult. You are "successful" – in monetary terms, anyway. And yet, you act like a spoiled child. A child that any mother would ground, take away privileges and put on restriction. A child that any parent would be embarrassed to take into public. So if we do not let our children behave this way, why do we let you, the adults behave this way? And what message is that sending to our children? How hypocritical are we in the eyes of our children? The eyes that will one day be in charge of our society. Is this what we want for them?

Today is the last day I will tolerate you and others like you. Today is the last day our society will make it okay for you to behave this way. Today, your permission is taken away. We do not give you permission to treat people disrespectfully. You may not yell at others because they are not in line with your own vision of yourself. You may not park and block others. You may not act like a crazy person and ruin the sports game for everyone present – especially your own children. You may not treat your spouse like a subordinate. You may not treat your subordinates at work as though they are somehow lesser than you. You may not treat people who work with you, socialize with you, and share the same space with you for even a brief moment, as anything less than equal. For if you do, when your permission runs out, you will regret it.

Repair the damage you've done. To those around you. To your children. To your friends. To your colleagues. To your subordinates. For if you don't you will be alone. And the world will continue on without you – and your unworthy behavior. No matter how loud you scream and rant and stomp your feet, "Don't you know who I am."

Pray for a Miracle

Recently, three Southern Californian women on their morning walk were struck down by a hit and run driver. Only one of them walked away. The other two are on life support and, if they recover, will most likely be completely paralyzed from the neck down. Each of these women in the hospital has three children. Children they will never again be able to care for. Children they will never again be able to pick up and hold. Children they will never be able to throw a ball to or sit down next to and help with a science project. These two women will not be able to volunteer in their child's classroom again. Will not be able to hug their husbands at the end of a long day. They will not be able to dance at their child's wedding.

My sister knows these three women. Last weekend at a soccer game, she spoke to the one who was lucky enough to walk away. She and many others are helping to care for the six children of the two women in the hospital. Everyone in their community is having a difficult time dealing with this tragedy. My sister has called me several times, very upset, feeling she must DO something. And she can't get a handle on why this has disrupted her life to such an extent. I didn't know these women, they are not from my town, but I too have been measurably disturbed by this event and it has altered my life and how I choose to live it. "Why?" my sister keeps asking. The realization is sobering. "Because it could have been you. Or me."

This one hit really close to home. Feel it. Learn from it and DO something. Hug your kid. Play ball with your kid. Make sure your husband knows you love him. Volunteer in your community. Be there. For your kids. For your husband. And for yourself. Because you never know when it can all be taken away.

This tragedy is almost impossible to comprehend because it is too painful, too close to home. Now is the time to pray for a miracle. For these women, for their children.

ADVICE ON BECOMING A MOTHER

Becoming a mother is the single most monumental and defining moment you will ever experience. You will see colors differently. Everything will take on a new hue and new meaning. Your priorities and boundaries will become more deeply defined with each passing moment. Your tolerance for the unacceptable wanes. You become a warrior - a warrior for your child, for you are their only voice. Motherhood is awe-inspiring. Here are the main points that I continually come upon in motherhood:

1. FOLLOW YOUR GUT. TRUST IT. NO MATTER WHAT "IMPRESSION" YOU MAY MAKE OR WHAT OTHERS MAY THINK. FOLLOW YOUR GUT.
2. YOU ARE YOUR KID'S FAVORITE TOY. ALL THEY NEED AND WANT IS YOU.
3. TRY AND LET EVERYTHING GO IN THE BEGINNING AND JUST FOCUS ON THE BABY. IT GOES SO FAST.
4. FOLLOW THROUGH ON WHAT YOU SAY. KIDS NEED CONSISTENCY AND BOUNDARIES.
5. KEEP A JOURNAL OR A CALENDAR AND MARK DOWN THINGS THAT HAPPEN. YOU WILL CHERISH THE NOTES A YEAR FROM NOW, AND EIGHT YEARS FROM NOW!

6. YES, YOU WILL BECOME ONE OF THOSE MOTHERS WHO LETS THEIR KIDS RUN WILD WHILE SINGLE PEOPLE / OLD PEOPLE / INTOLERANT PEOPLE LOOK ON IN SCORN. HELP THEM REMEMBER THAT SOMEONE ONCE CHANGED THEIR POOPY DIAPERS, TOO.
7. WHEN TAKING PHOTOS, GET CLOSE, THEN GET CLOSER.
8. NOW THAT YOU HAVE AN OFFICIAL MOTHERHOOD PERMIT, AND ALL THE RESPONSIBILITIES THEREBY INCLUDED, YOUR PERMIT FOR CLEANING THE HOUSE, DOING LAUNDRY, WASHING THE CAR, OPERATING A LAWNMOWER, AND ANYTHING ELSE YOU WON'T HAVE TIME FOR HAS BEEN OFFICIALLY REVOKED. FIND SOMEONE ELSE TO DO THESE THINGS FOR YOU.
9. EVEN IF YOU HAVE A BAD VOICE, SING.
10. REMEMBER, WHEN POTTY TRAINING, ANYWHERE OTHER THAN IN THE DIAPERS IS PROGRESS.
11. PICK YOUR BATTLES.
12. DON'T FORGET THAT THIS IS ALL NEW FOR YOUR HUSBAND, AND HE IS GOING THROUGH A LOT OF EMOTIONS, TOO.

Litter Bugs

Where do the boundaries of your home end? The walls of your house? Your property line? Your street? For me, my home extends to the places I frequent, the places I take my kids, my neighborhood, my city, my world. I try my hardest to treat these places and the people I encounter with the same respect that I would in my own home.

Driving along Ventura Boulevard recently, my kids and I witnessed a man throw his entire bag of fast food trash out the window of his moving car. "Did you see that?" My kids gasped! They know it's wrong to litter, why didn't an adult? At their insistence, I picked up my cell and called the 800 number displayed on the side of his vehicle. (Brilliant.) After politely saying hello, I asked if he was driving on Ventura, (to verify it was him), and upon confirmation, informed him that my family lives in the neighborhood that he just littered in and would he would please treat our city with more respect. There was a long, silent, awkward pause. Finally he said, "You're right. I apologize. It was wrong, I won't do it again." This was not an unpleasant exchange. It was simply pointing out the obvious to someone - that their behavior affects those around them. My kids felt like they had changed their world for the better.

At least they felt that way until our next unfortunate litter encounter while sitting on the patio of our local Starbucks. A businessman in a red Corvette threw his cigarette box wrapping out the window – in front of everyone on the patio. My kids once again gasped. Their mouths gaping –

mouthing to me, "Did you see that?" Of course, I did. But truthfully, I was tired and just wanted to let it go. But my kids could not let it go. As the adults, we must set appropriate examples so that all hell does not break loose one day. So, as he pulled out, I got the man's attention and politely stated that he 'dropped' something from his car. He was not as gracious as our previous encounter. After a heated outburst on his side, I was so stunned I could only reply, "So you think you are above everyone else?" "Yes, I do," he said. "I pay rent for this building and I can do whatever I want." Evidently, he was the owner of the phone store next to Starbucks and could care less about the people who frequented this shopping center or those that lived in the neighborhood. How do you reach someone like that? By choosing not to support his business?

When did it become okay to litter again? At our freeway off-ramp we witnessed a black Passat with three young adults in it throw bags, cups and crushed paper out their window. At this point all we could do was shake our heads. It was then that we noticed our off-ramp is littered with trash. Even our neighborhood streets were not absent of trash in the gutters. The kids and I decided to clean it up on our next walk. With grab sticks and trash bags we picked up litter and pushed a shopping cart to an appropriate place. We felt we had done our part that day to make our home - our extended home - better for everyone who visits. Our home stretches far beyond our property lines. How far does yours stretch? It can stretch as far as you allow it. See you at home.

Safety Mom

Without guidelines and rules, our world would be mayhem.

While some might live well and thrive in chaos, children flourish best with defined boundaries.

With expectations and consistency.

With the adults acting like adults and modeling appropriate behavior.

Trusting that the adults will take care of the kids.

All the kids.

Your kids.

My kids.

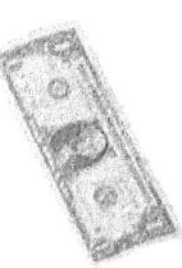

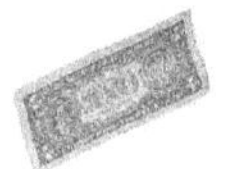

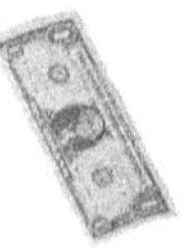

Playdate Safety

Why do we give up for an afternoon that which is most precious and valuable to us – our children - to people we don't know very well without asking any questions?

Why do we let our children get into someone's car and go to someone's house that we have never driven with or been to? Because we want our children to make friends.

But as parents, we must not be afraid to ask questions. Our children count on us to keep them safe, whether we are with them or not. So ask the questions, and then make your own determination as to what level of safety is right for you, your child and your family.

May I come with my child? If the answer is "No" to this first question, do not let your child go to this person's house.

Ask for an exchange of pertinent information: last name, address, home phone and cell phone numbers. And teach your child your cell phone number. This is often more important than your home number, for chances are if you are not with your child, you are not at home.

Do you use booster seats? If this parent is going to drive your child make sure that the booster seats are appropriate to your child, or better yet, use your own.

Indicate any food, pet, medicinal or other allergies your child may have. You never know what children may encounter in someone else's home.

Do you have a pool? Is it fenced?

Do you have a trampoline? Is there a safety net around it?

Do you allow your children to close and lock their doors? To allow for proper supervision, it is very important to insist upon an open door playdate policy.

Do you have guns in your house? If you are okay with this, probe further to ensure that they are responsible gun owners. Are the guns assembled? Are the guns and ammunitions locked in separate cabinets? Do your children know you have guns in your house? Where are the guns? Where is the ammunition?

Are you CPR and first aid certified? If your child chokes on a chip or piece of apple, or hits his/her head you want to know that the adult present can properly handle a stressful situation.

Do you have dogs or any other animals? If your child is afraid of animals, ask if they can be caged during the playdate.

Do you have older siblings? What are their ages? Will they be home while my child is at your home?

Will there be any other adults present while my child is at your home? This includes babysitters, construction workers, housekeepers, gardeners, adult friends, husbands and/or business associates. Know whom your child will be exposed to.

What is the level of supervision? If the parent is going to be working in a home office and distracted during the playdate, you need to know this.

Is the babysitter going to be the only one supervising the children? If yes, get to know her.

There are many ways to have this conversation without breaking out a list and conducting an interrogation. Be open to the giving and receiving of this type of information. It makes everyone more comfortable, and establishes a relationship between parents that could potentially last for years to come if your children become good friends.

Be Prepared

My 8-year son choked on cheese. We were at a pizza restaurant with friends sitting at two tables - an adult table and an adjacent kid table. I felt a tapping on my shoulder and turned to find my son straining for air, though none was available to him. He could not even cough. His face was bright red, eyes full of fear, mouth strained in an oval and neck muscles pushing, trying to dislodge the cheese. His fingers were wet with saliva and a small hunk of cheese – he had tried to get it out himself, but only succeeded in lodging it further down. I took this all in within a nanosecond. Then I was up on my feet performing the heimlick maneuver on him. Twice. A large chunk of melted cheese flew out onto the floor.

My son curled up onto me as we sat back down, both of us shaking. After a bit, he got up and returned to his friends. I was still shaking. I could still see his face staring at me to help him.

I turned back to my table of friends who were visibly upset as well. "I don't think I would know what to do in that situation," said one of my friends. Others nodded in agreement. I stared back at them, grateful that I was here for my child. Fortunately I had recertified my CPR and First Aid training last summer. And while that does not guarantee appropriate action in a choking situation, it does arm you with the knowledge of how to do it. And that knowledge could save your child's life. Or someone else's child who happens to be in your care.

So consider having all caregivers (including dads, grandparents, nannies, other moms who watch your children, babysitters, teachers, coaches, etc.) take a class in CPR and First Aid. For information on finding a program right for you and your family, call the American Red Cross or Google "CPR" for other options.

Care for a Knowledge Booster?

Regardless of age, the California Highway Patrol and the American Academy of Pediatrics recommends that for optimum safety your child should be in a booster seat until they are 80 pounds and (not or) 4'9" tall (that's 57 inches). According to the National Highway Traffic Safety Administration all children 12 and under should be restrained in the rear seat. The back seat placement reduces the chance of injury or death to your child by 30% as compared to the front seat, regardless of whether or not your car has an airbag.

Are we in such a hurry for our kids to grow up that we will forsake their safety? Let's not forget that just because our kids may know their alphabet, can add, multiply or recite the Pythagorean theorem, they are still our babies. Seat belts are made for adults and don't fit properly until a person weighs 80 pounds and is 4'9" tall. The car manufacturers do not make safety belts with small children in mind, which is why we have child safety seat laws. And often times the laws are slow to catch up. A few years ago the law was changed because the lawmakers realized that 4 years old and forty pounds was not enough to keep our children safe. So even though your child should be 80 pounds and (not or) 4'9" tall, the actual law, as posted by the CHP states: "Children must be secured in an appropriate child passenger restraint (safety seat or booster seat) until they are at least 6 years old or weigh at least 60 pounds." And all children under 16 must be properly buckled. The cost of a violation is $270 and a point on your driving record.

On a recent kindergarten school field trip to the Pumpkin Patch several other adults and I who volunteered to supervise were surprised by the improper usage of car seats and boosters. I had a conversation with a few of the mothers about their safety seats and they honestly did not know they were using them inappropriately. So here are a few guidelines supported by the AAP, the CHP and Safety BeltSafe USA:

Always place children in the back seat of a car.

If your child cannot sit for the entire car ride all the way against the back of the seat with knees bending comfortably at the edge of the seat and the lap belt touching thighs and the shoulder belt crossing the shoulder between the neck and the arm, then your child needs to be in a booster. This usually coincides with reaching 80 pounds and 4'9" in height.

If your car's back seat is lower than your child's ears, use a high back booster seat to protect your child's head and neck.

If your car's back seat is higher than your child's ears (most likely there will be a headrest), you may use a backless booster seat.

Boosters must be used in conjunction with both the shoulder and lap belt.

Your child's safety seat should be no less than 5 years old. It should be destroyed and discarded if it is more than 10 years old. Please dispose of it properly so that no one can find it and use it. Also, do not buy used car seats as you would not be able to verify the age of the seat or if its integrity has been compromised due to an accident.

If your child's safety seat has been in an accident, you must discard and destroy it. Your car insurance will cover the cost of new seats as part of your accident claim.

Find out if your child's safety seat has been recalled. Go to http://carseat.org/recalls.

So why are so many kids not in boosters? Or appropriate boosters? Do they think they are too old? Is it not cool? Do their parents not know enough to know better or is it just too inconvenient to schlep that thing around?

Or is it the name? Booster? Does it sound like a baby item? So let's call them 'risers'. I personally know of small adults that use 'risers' in their own cars. Why? Because seat belts do not fit properly unless you are 80 pounds and (not or) 4'9" tall, regardless of age.

Our children rely on us to keep them safe. Don't be afraid to demand your kids and other kids ride in booster seats in your car, for you, the one behind the wheel, are ultimately responsible for the safety of all children in your car. Even driving a couple of blocks home you must use boosters. Most accidents occur near your place of residence. According to the AAP, "motor vehicle crashes are the number one cause of death for children and adolescents ages 1 to 21." And it is not just your driving that you have to worry about - it is the drunk driver who loses control and slams into your car full of children. My children. Your children. Our children. Their chances of walking away from that accident just mere blocks from your house are much greater if they are properly buckled. If the seat belt fits them properly. If they are in a booster. Or a riser. Or whatever you want to call it.

So help me make it the norm that kids ride in proper safety seats in any car. Make the parent who does not use boosters or risers the one who has to be embarrassed to say she doesn't, not the kids and parents who do use them. For we are not the uncool ones, we are the ones who are putting our child's and your child's safety first. We are the parents who have a better chance at ensuring our family remains safe and sound, even if we are just driving down the street to school.

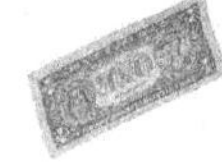

Sexy Mama

This is the meagerest of the meager in the scrap department.

This is the plate that is licked clean.

Where there is so little left I wonder how it ever began.

But on occasion, one juicy tidbit is tossed in and that somehow feeds this need for a long, long, (sigh), long time.

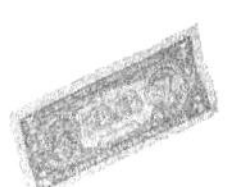

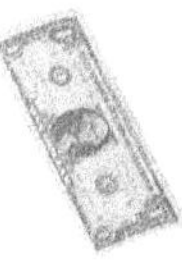

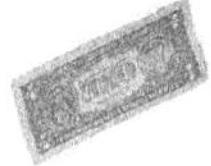

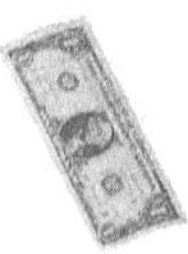

I Lost My Smile to Botox

It's official. I have become a desperate suburban housewife. How? I actually agreed to attend a Botox party with my dear friend, I'll call her Mrs. Jones, and wound up with a botched botulism job that has changed my face – and not for the better. My friend had heard about the party and RSVP'd for the both of us. As it was taking place in the evening during the week, we were elated at the opportunity to escape the homework/dinner/bedtime routine, so we hired a babysitter, put on heels, and headed out. Upon entering the party, I felt so ridiculously L.A, so sadly suburban, as I was witness to women of various ages holding icepacks to red swollen faces, balancing plates of catered food, and chit chatting away as though they were at an actual cocktail party and this behavior was completely normal. I penned my name on the sign in sheet and Mrs. Jones and I looked around for what to do next. We were disappointed that there were no cocktails – we were in heels after all! Evidently, the invitation had indicated that there would be, and upon complaint, the office manager confessed to Mrs. Jones that she was nursing a hangover and just couldn't bring herself to be around booze again so soon. She did offer to reimburse us if we'd like to run out to a liquor store and bring it back with a receipt. Mrs. Jones and I thought about it for a moment, but decided that kind of behavior would be just too blatantly desperate.

Mrs. Jones and I made small talk with the others present. I recognized one woman, but could not place her. I almost did not want to say anything to her for I didn't want the word out that I was having Botox done. But hey, she was here, too, right? She must be having Botox as well. Turns out her kids play at the same baseball field as my youngest son and that she was only here to accompany her friend as she could not imagine sticking a needle containing botulism in her face. Ah well, so much for our budding friendship – her inherent judgment on my shallow impending behavior ended any hope of further conversation.

Thankfully a young nurse called me into a room. Mrs. Jones and I went in together – that's what all the suburban housewives do, don't you know, as beauty treatments have become a team sport. The doctor came in – the only man in the entire place – and looked carefully at Mrs. Jones' face. Together they both decided on two areas – forehead and around the eyes. The nurse - with no wrinkles, rosasea, brown spots or pimples, quietly left to retrieve the vials. One vial for the forehead. One for around the eyes. About fifteen pricks later, my friend sat in front of me with little mounds of botulism protruding all over her face. She held a skinny ice pack to them, and moved to my chair as I hopped up on the table. "Same for me," I said, not to be outdone by Mrs. Jones. Ha! Who would bother with only one area? The young, handsome doctor looked closely at my face and asked me to smile hard. Then frown hard. The nurse came back yet again with two more vials and in-between frowning hard and smiling hard, needles were stuck into my face so that I wouldn't be able to frown hard or smile hard anymore.

Freshly poked, I took my ice pack and rotated it around my face. The forehead. Left eye area. Right eye area. Then again, in the same order, trying to give each area equal time. I felt a bit obsessive about it. I wanted to make sure I did it right – to get my money's worth. Mrs. Jones and I rejoined the party, making small talk with strangers as we moved the ice packs into different positions on our face. Finally, one by one, the ice packs we held and those held by the other women present, started to melt and drip and had to be thrown out. It was a very odd scene indeed. And no one really addressed it. When did this behavior become so widely accepted that we can't even poke fun at ourselves whilst in the middle of it? I felt a bit like I was participating in a scene from the 1980's movie, Brazil.

One nice older woman in her mid sixties had also come with a friend and stated proudly that the doctor told her she did not have "Botox issues."

Please. As we rolled our eyes, her friend jumped right in and told us what her issues were, "Well, she needs this, this and this," she said. Just like a true friend.

As we said our goodbyes, the manager doled out party favors. Party favors have come a long way. They are not just for kids anymore. Any semblance of a party evidently requires party favors. Is this to make us feel younger too? Don't party favors come after cake, ice cream and an off tune rendition of Happy Birthday to little Betty? This one included a pink t-shirt with BOTOX written in crystal studs across the front, a key chain, a mirror, and some skin care products to try. Mrs. Jones insisted she would never wear the shirt. "It's good for gardening," I said. She gave me a hard look. Right. She has a gardener for that. Don't we all? (Yes, I know this sounds elitist and shallow, but that's the point of this article, hello?)

Days went by and I kept frowning hard and smiling hard. Nothing seemed different. Then, about seven days after the needles were stuck into my face, I caught a glimpse of myself smiling in a mirror. Except I looked like I was saying "Ewwwwww," not smiling. The corners of my mouth wouldn't turn up. I kept trying to force a smile, to 'smile hard' but my smile would barely move. In fact, at this point, three weeks later, I can't really smile at all. My smile now looks like I am smelling something disgusting.

The next morning after this horrifying turn of events, I met Mrs. Jones at the gym. One must also have a good physique to compete in the world of the Jones'. I demonstrated over and over again to her my 'new' smile. She said she wouldn't have noticed if I didn't point it out. "It's like if you gain four pounds, no one really notices but you," she stated. Yeah, right. I know her too well. That was no help. Still, I wondered if I was being too critical of my own face and the Botox process. I looked again. Tried smiling. Nope. Not being too critical. This face-saving beauty product has changed the way I smile – again, not for the better.

I started looking around at nearly every woman's face that I came into contact with. Looking for signs of 'work.' I started listening carefully to conversations. One woman just had Radiesse injected in her wrinkles. One just had Botox in her forehead. These were women I don't know very well, yet here they were telling me their beauty secrets. I guess these aren't secrets after all. Still, I am not telling anyone, only you. I've come to realize that very few people would ever notice my odd smile because the "Ewwwwww" smile is the new smile on many female faces these days.

So, I lost my smile to Botox, but at least I got the t-shirt – and I will wear it while I garden. And at least it isn't permanent. Thank goodness it only lasts for a few months. This experience has been a good lesson for me in keeping up with the Jones'. We all want to look our best, but for whom? Really? My husband noticed that my smile had changed, but he did not say anything until after he read the first draft of this article. "Why didn't you say something?" I asked, a bit irritated at his silence. "Because I did not want to make you self conscious," he gently replied. He is a truly wonderful man, and that small sentence proved to me that what I need to work on keeping up with are those things that really matter - my marriage, my family, my friends, and my community. Not the new definition of beauty as defined by the society around me. So, having realized that, am I redeemed for my ridiculously shallow behavior? Even if I do it again?

This is the "ewwwww" smile. Do you think a lesson was learned?

Flirty Fingers

The first time I ever experienced (and thus, was confused by) a 'text' acronym known amongst the text messaging savvy, was from a business associate I did not know well, but who signed off an email with "LOL". 'Lot's of love?" I said out loud a bit flabbergasted. At that point, we'd had several phone conversations and knew him to be an attractive man (he also has his photo on the bottom of all correspondence) I felt this was terribly inappropriate and much too familiar - not at all professional. In a befuddled state I actually called Kelsie, my thirteen-year old niece, to translate it for me. And believe me, during that conversation, she did LOL - Laugh Out Loud - at me. (If I had an emoticon I would insert the one with the pink blushing cheeks right here.)

Since that time, it seems that I have been inundated with people who only want to IM (instant message) or text. No one wants to talk on the phone anymore. Why? Because they can secretly do it in front of other people without anyone really knowing - at a business meeting, in the movies, in a class, at dinner? Hmm. A whole different level of rudeness is brewing. This one though, is sneaky. At least if you answer your phone in front of me I can choose to mock you, walk away in disdain, or on rare occasion, tolerate it.

Eventually I, (I must embarrassingly admit - insert gasping emoticon here) got caught up in it. I got an IM address. Just so you know, I often spend my days holed up in my office writing or schlepping kids, so to have instant 'human' contact all day seemed fabulous. And seeing those little bubbles popping up from people who were my 'buddies' – albeit people I would not normally talk to on a daily basis – made me feel very social. Except after a while, not so much. It was still just me sitting alone in my office not actually talking or having 'human' contact, but I was receiving and giving TMI. My suggestions for phone conversations were snuffed. My IM and text buddies did not want to talk to me. They only wanted to IM and text me. It took me a while to realize this, but not until the conversations had deteriorated into outright inappropriateness. As though because we are all so isolated by our technological objects, there is an unannounced permission to do and say, with your fingers, whatever you please, IMO. And it was fun, for a while. Then it just bordered on wrong, and finally for me, it was no longer okay. There's got to be a line, even in texting. EIE. The same line that exists at a cocktail party – a harmless repartee is ok, but 'finger flirting' as I call it goes beyond harmless and becomes downright offensive. And I just HIWTH.

So do not LOL at me. I am going dark. AAMAOF, if u r reading this, then that is part of the problem. ATM I am declaring my text and chat life over. IOW, I want to deal with human beings again. My fingers are tired of doing the talking. And DQMOT, but there is so much being said, er, communicated via anything other that our voices, that we seem to have lost them. The words flying wirelessly via our phones and computers ride the line of tasteless most of the time. WIT? Because of the barrier. It makes it feel safe to say things you wouldn't say in person or on the phone. GOK I have gotten myself into a load of crud by chatting. It got out of control. And while it W4M for while, I realize that it's 2 easy. And ultimately that makes it 2 hard.

CMIIW, but I'll bet that most of us have IM'd or texted (is that even a word?) something we later regretted. Something we would not have said out loud. But did so in the moment with an acronym because it felt safe, oddly anonymous, and ITFA they aren't real words. After all we are not really saying anything real. Right? BION, that is just stupid. Because then it's not just been said, it's in writing, and a good percentage of the general population knows how to translate 'text'. So while in the moment you may have a BEG on your face, the cringing comes later. Trust me. I know.

So, if you want to talk to me. TALK to me. F2F. Or FT2T, pick up the phone. Better yet, knock on my door. Get rid of that GD glowing screen in your face and GAL. Why is it so much easier to look at than a human face? And once you are with me, keep that flirty thing it in your pocket and in its case and away from me. And I pray that when you actually try to have human contact you don't fail. So, GOWI already. DTRT. I am. YOYO. TTFN.

Need a key to get it? I love you more already! FWIW.

LOL = laugh out loud

IM = instant message

TMI = too much information

IMO = in my opinion

EIE = enough is enough

HIWTH = hate it when that happens

AAMAOF = as a matter of fact

ATM = at this moment

IOW = in other words

DQMOT - don't quote me on this

WIT = why is that?

GOK = God only knows

W4M = works for me

CMIIW = call me if I'm wrong

ITFA = in the final analysis

BION = believe it or not

BEG = big evil grin

F2F = face to face

FT2T = from time to time

GD = goddamn

GAL = get a life

GOWI = get on with it

DTRT = do the right thing

YOYO = you're on your own

TTFN = ta ta for now

FWIW = for what it's worth

Cute Dad List

"Your husband looks soooo cute today!" My eyes widened at this woman's observation. I looked over at Keith as yet as another woman commented, "He always does, he is so on the Cute Dad List."

I tried to furrow my brow (no one really can anymore due to the brilliance of Botox). I did not feel I knew these women well enough for them to be making these remarks about my husband in front of me. They were not in my inner circle. Which means that my husband is being noticed outside my circle, outside my realm of consciousness. I felt proud and agitated and defensive all at the same time. "Who else is on your Cute Dad List?" I wanted to know, hoping their answers would somehow clarify their intentions.

This gaggle of women, again barely known to me, proceeded to list those dads that if I had a list (and of course, I do now) would be on mine. This made me oddly nervous. And excited. My husband is on the Cute Dad List. Then it occurred to me.... I have the same taste in men as these women. Hmmm. Better to leave our relationship as it is – fairly non-existent. I quickly sidled up to my husband and ushered him away.

A few days later and back within the safety of my inner circle, I discussed the concept of the Cute Dad List. My inner circle consists of a few fabulous women, ranging in age from early thirties to late fifties, who all have differing but strong personalities and a range of kids - some boys, some girls. They represent different religious views, from Catholic, Jewish and Agnostic, to Spiritual and everything in between. And, most importantly to this conversation, a wide range of husband types exist among us. Most of us cross paths weekly on some level and several times of year we congregate at the same parties with our spouses.

One of my dearest friends, Mrs. Jones, (you may remember her from my botched Botox experience), had, of course, her pick of the husbands already in her mind. Mrs. Smith, another dear friend, was a bit surprised to know that it was her husband who was on the top of Mrs. Jones' list. Yep, that was an awkward moment.

The conversation became a bit even more uncomfortable as we all realized it is each other's husbands that are now on our respective newly created Cute Dad Lists. I suddenly realized why the women I did not know well enough had chosen my husband, and why they felt safe enough to tell me this tidbit of information. Because I don't socialize with them and it will never become an issue - unlike the now oddly established relationships between Mrs. Jones and Mr. Smith or Mrs. Smith and Mr. Boyle. (All names have been changed to protect the identity of my inner circle and to alleviate any grief I may receive for letting this proverbial cat out of its respective bag. Suffice it to say that I know the Jones, the Smiths, the Longs, the Marks, and the Boyles very, very well. And will be referring to them often).

Realizing the prickly tension building during this conversation would not serve me well, I branched out and named a few gorgeous dads I know of, but that none of us really actually know, to put on the top of my list. Interestingly, all of them have athletic bodies. Another dear friend in our inner circle, Mrs. Long, seems to always gravitate toward the same type as her husband. Boring. (Sorry, Mrs. Long. Just my opinion). That which I gravitate toward couldn't be more varied and different from Keith, my husband. A few of the inner circle women refused to claim anyone on their list that wasn't in the "inner circle" husband community. Telling. Very telling. Not a conversation that one would forget the next time anyone in the inner circle may have had a wee bit too much sauce at a gathering. Husband or wife. Because you can bet each and every husband of the women in my inner circle knows what was said. And whom we all chose. Some things are not sacred. Although, I wonder if they told their husbands whom they chose. I can name two that probably did not. Again, telling. Hmmm.

I encourage you not to build a Cute Dad List within your close group of friends. And if you choose to ignore this piece of advice, at least set ground rules. Make sure you are not allowed to name anyone else's husband within your group. Keep a sense of "this will never happen" to heighten the excitement (or at least pretend this is what would heighten it for you). Otherwise it hits too close to home. I realize I will never socialize with the women that were pining after my husband that day. Perhaps if they had never said anything we might have become good friends. But not now. He is mine. He is my kids' Cute Dad. Keep your grubby paws off.

Keith is a very Cute Dad!

Oscar High Friends

George Clooney touched my face. Seriously. Everyone I tell this to reacts the same, "Nuh-uh," as my 13 year-old niece might say. But it's true! I got onto an elevator at the Kodak Theatre after the Oscar telecast was finished and as I turned around to face the front of the elevator and stare up at the numbers like we all do, George Clooney and his girlfriend, Sarah Larson walked on.

The doors closed right after them, and all of a sudden I was mute. I glanced at Keith, wide eyed, "Oh my God!" was what I wanted to shout! After that initial awkward elevator pause, Sarah mentioned that her dress was heavy. "It's beautiful," I remarked wanting to engage them both in conversation. We only had four floors to go up! So I stammered, "I will never again buy a gown that ties around my neck – it's killing me!" Both George and Sarah looked at my neck as I dramatically tugged at the strings. "It's really red," George said. "Does it hurt?" Sarah asked. Then, it happened. "It also looks like somebody tagged you," George said lifting his right arm toward me, and then gently, with great care, he rubbed away on my left cheek what appeared to him to be a lipstick mark. As though someone had kissed my cheek there. Only, no one had. To this day I am sure no one had. But he saw something and felt the need to "fix" me, and I let him. The elevators door opened. I thanked him (I think), he smiled and walked off with Sarah. I don't remember if I said anything else as they were walking away. All kinds of things went through my mind – everything from the mundane to the outright obnoxious.

But before I could gather my wits, the elevator was on its way down – their floor was not our floor. Again I turned to Keith and this time was able to say out-loud, "Oh my God! George Clooney just stroked my face!" Keith laughed. Then the woman who had witnessed the whole thing – the woman whose job it was that night to be the elevator attendant – broke her silence, "You don't know him?" she asked in pure awe. "No!" I replied. "I thought for sure you all were good friends," she continued. It was then that I saw her face for the first time, and on her face was the realization that the brief exchange she witnessed by what she assumed were people well known to each other and to others - the comparing of dresses, the oddly intimate way George rubbed lipstick off my cheek, the smiles and courtesies – was actually between complete strangers...and that it could have happened to her. She was flabbergasted at that possibility. In that moment, I saw my own reaction in her and shared the moment.

Let me just say that I am not a "star struck" person. I have attended several events surrounded by countless celebrities. I actually even know a few. For the most part, they are just people who want the same things you and I (the ordinary people) do. Obviously there are exceptions, and on Oscar night I had to make one of my own. I became star struck, not in the moment, but after the moment was over. I was practically giddy. I called a girlfriend. And another. And then I called my mom and dad. I just had to share that George Clooney touched my face! (This behavior is very uncharacteristic of me).

But as I reflect on the event after some time has passed (a whole three days), I realize that the four of us - me, George, Sarah and Keith - shared a common moment that evening. We experienced a sameness, if you will, in where we were and what we were experiencing, thus, a brief bond of acceptance and equality was created.

So now, I consider us friends (No, I am not a stalker, just a little off my rocker). George is obviously very tender and caring and Sarah is very funny and approachable. And of course, both are even better looking in person. What else could anyone want in new friends? So, George and Sarah, if you are reading this, feel free to contact me. I'd love to have you over for dinner. I make a mean Spaghetti sauce.

Naughty Yoga

Due to the publicity for the new exercise craze, the S Factor, and the fact that they just opened one in the Valley, I decided I had to try it. A bit bashful to try it on my own – it is strip dancing and pole dancing after all – I arranged for a 'mom's night out' event. Me and four of my friends wound up attending. The introductory class is two hours and we all came in workout clothes not really knowing what to expect.

Our expectations changed when we walked in and there were hot pants, short fluffy skirts, and 6-inch platforms for sale where sweat pant and tanks would normally be. Our instructor walked in to the waiting room, and with a very guttural and exuberant "Yeeeeaaaaahhhh" she welcomed us all to the S Factor. We followed her back into a dimly lit room. Wood floors, 3 poles. The poles were intimidating. Like 7th grade gym class when you had to climb to the top of the rope to pass (do you think they still do that?) The instructor laid out yoga mats in an oval around the poles. She dimmed the lights even more and turned on music. The music was great – songs you know but never really listen to because you don't know who the artist is or because your kids are always around. Great sensual beats and lyrics. I wish I could remember them.

Anyway, with another guttural and now naughty sounding, "Yeeee-aaaaahhhh!" our instructor talked us through an hour of floor work. "Close your eyes and move slower, Slow the f--- down....Slower. Now, start to touch yourself with your hands, let them trail your body. You're gorgeous."

I think most people were peeking at this point. Feeling a bit awkward and wondering just how slow are we supposed to be going and exactly how are we supposed to touch ourselves? She led us through stretches that were akin to yoga – only naughty yoga, with names like "Open your candy shop". Some elicited much laughter – especially the naughty version of downward dog – "drag your chest on the floor and stick that beautiful ass in the air."

It was at this point that we all realized that the slower you went and more you stuck your ass in the air, oddly, the better you looked. After the floor work, we moved on to being taught "The Walk". Again, in slow motion, we stuck our butts out, chest up, and slowly, slowly (slowly is so key in naughty yoga) dragged our feet and crossed them in front of the leg in front, sinking into our hips. And, if you were so inclined and not bashful as all eyes were open now, touch yourself with your hands up and down your body as you walked.

Now, as a person in relatively good shape, and for how slow we were actually moving the entire time, I was surprised how shaky my muscles were, surprised I could feel the beginning of soreness. Who knew, stripping works a whole different set of muscles than TaeBo and "regular" yoga. After the walking lesson, we moved to the last lesson – and I believe what most of us were actually there to try – the pole. After many "Yeaeeeeaaaahhhhs and discussions about how it doesn't really matter how you look on the pole if when you hit the bottom you get up slowly (again, the key), butt first way up in the air and, you guessed it, slowly rise. And damn if she wasn't right.

So all these white suburban moms trying to spin awkwardly on a pole looked a bit odd, but a few stuck their asses out and rose up slowly and damn if that is not what you remember! Inhibitions started to ease and most were wanting to try the pole again. Then our instructor changed (in front of the class!) into skimpy hot pants and demonstrated a routine for us. We all sat along the wall. I felt like I was at the Frisky Kitty. We were all mesmerized by the slow naughty movements we had just learned being made into a 'dance' routine. And her skill on the pole was impressive. Especially now knowing first hand how painful it is if you do it wrong.

As I watched the class watching her, I wondered, how many of these women have actually been to a real strip club? And is this their way of living out that fantasy and making it okay? One woman confided that she had two small kids under the age of five. She was there for husband. Or was she? And truthfully, why was I there? I really enjoyed the sensual permission to use my body as an erotic messenger (not my words, but I like them). To watch others use theirs as such and to dream of actually learning a routine to dance my naughty yoga dance for someone else. But, unless you are a suburban mom, in my inner circle or a complete stranger in a dimly lit class, I can all but guarantee, you will not see it. I move way too slow.

Nothing to Catch

When approached to write an article about getting caught while having sex, I excitedly agreed. After all, I had a funny story of my three-year-old jumping on my husband's back during the act. "Why are you so sweaty, Dada? Are you and Mama wrestling?" But I couldn't write it. I started to dread this assignment, not even able to come up with an opening sentence. I felt dead to the subject and I couldn't figure out why. I tried to ignore it but couldn't. After two weeks struggling to think of something to write, the truth hit me while driving home during rush hour on the 101. And it stung. I'd have to face the facts, admit to someone else and to myself for that matter (on paper!), that in maintaining the status quo of my world, the sexual part of my life was over. That my marriage was nearly over. That my husband and I had no sex life. That he did not want me. That I did not want him. That the growing chasm between us became more insurmountable as each day passed. That although we still had to work together, parent together and live in the same house together, we were no longer living in the same room, much less sharing the same bed. We did not – and had not for quite some time – want to be together. I felt like I'd been kicked in the gut. All of a sudden I couldn't breathe. I had to pull the car over to the side of the road as the sadness overwhelmed me. There in the shade of a strange tree, I wept. Wept for what was. Wept for what I wanted and couldn't have. What I needed and couldn't figure out a way to get. Wept because I hadn't been able to in so long. I eventually pulled myself together, but after this initial dam broke, my emotions would sneak up on me and overtake me regardless of where I was. Isolating myself from my family and friends was the only way I knew how to cope. I couldn't face anyone during this emotional breakdown. Then one very polite and controlled evening watching television on the sofa, my husband asked if we were just going to ignore tomorrow. "Tomorrow?" I asked, thinking I had missed some work deadline or kids' soccer game. "Our anniversary," he replied. And there it was again. The deep sadness welling to the surface. But this time I didn't hold it in. The anger and resentment toward him dimmed and the memories of what had been good, what had worked, and of the love we once had shared for each other, overwhelmed me instead of the sadness. I loved this man, my husband. I still do. I needed him. And in this moment I let him be there for me and allowed myself to be there for him. We kissed. And cried. And made love. There was still something there, something worth saving, worth working for. And maybe in time we'll be able to worry once again about trying not to get caught in the act.

Media Shame

In a letter to the editor of the magazine, Marie Clare, dated May 5, 2006, I wrote:

Leslie (who was editor at the time),

I am an avid reader of Marie Claire. I am also a mother to two children. And while your magazine does a wonderful job of bringing women's' issues across the globe to the forefront, your May 2006 issue perpetuates a stereotype fought everyday everywhere in America - Mothers don't have to be frumpy, stressed out envious women!!! On page 155 you show a glamorous model strutting down a sidewalk while an unkempt, unmade up, distraught looking mother with a baby and stroller obviously "wishes" she could change places with her.

Shame on Marie Clare. Yes, motherhood is overwhelming, but it has changed. We take care of our kids and ourselves. We workout, we dress well, we do our hair and make up, we do what we can to make the world a better place for our kids - and others - through work, volunteerism, and activism in our own community and also through the programs in your magazine. It is insulting to see you portray a mother in this manner. Especially during the month of May when Mothers across the globe are to be celebrated.

The mothers I know are the gorgeous, well-dressed, fabulous women strutting their stuff on the sidewalk. And yes, sometimes that "stuff" is a kid (or two) and a stroller, but it adds to our power as women, not diminishes it.

Kathleen Melton

Hot, Stylish Mom

Home Stretch

Excerpts from Kathleen Melton's column in the Los Angeles Daily News

Your house is your main environment.

You have a relationship with it, just as you do anything else.

How's that working for you?

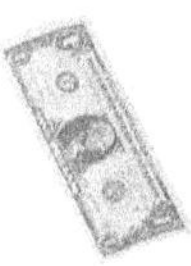

Kitchen Appliances vs. Fall Fashion

The last thing I want to spend my limited extra discretionary budget on is appliances. It's fall, after all, and I saw this fabulous new pair of boots the other day.... But, alas, my dishwasher and my refrigerator are on their last legs. Both are at least nine years old, as that is how long I have owned my house, and I believe they were actually purchased in '94, making them lucky thirteen. And yes, while thirteen years is a long life for an appliance, that doesn't make me feel any better about having to spend money on new ones. Did I mention the boots?

Reluctantly, I set out with my two boys and Keith to buy two new appliances. Misery loves company. I had the model numbers and even the dimensions of my now defunct existing models, and was prepared to spend around $3,500. I figured two grand-plus for a good fridge, and one grand for a high-end dishwasher. The extra five hundred was padding to cushion the blow of what the reality may be, having not shopped for appliances in over a decade.

And I must mention that both my dishwasher and my refrigerator have "cabinet" façades – meaning they have the same cabinet treatment on their faces as the rest of the kitchen so they "blend" in, a very popular decorating style in the mid nineties.

Imagine my shock, dismay and surprise when I discovered that dishwashers are no longer made in two sections, like mine. They are now one long face front or a drawer. This rendered my cabinet façade for a dishwasher useless. The size of my refrigerator is also no longer manufactured, rendering not just the cabinet façade useless, but quite possible the hole in the middle of my cabinets where it currently sits in my kitchen.

Speechless. I looked at the sales person. I looked at Keith. I looked at my kids who were 'Heely-ing' around bored out of their minds. "You're kidding, right?" This was all I could manage. He explained the new designs. "So everyone who has my type of dishwasher and refrigerator is going to have to completely reconfigure their kitchen space because the manufacturers no longer make products this size or style?"

What a scam. But by whom? The contractors who will be called to rearrange holes, cabinets, and create new false façades for these new appliances? By the appliance manufacturers? I don't want a big black/white/stainless or matte gold fridge in my kitchen. I just want a new one I can use my cabinet panels on!

Within the two hours that we were appliance shopping, I went from spending $3500 (that I really don't have) on appliances to completely remodeling our kitchen to include an island with two dishwasher drawers, reconfiguring cabinets to accommodate a side by side fridge/freezer, demolishing a bar in the family room to make up for the lost space in the kitchen, and, well, we might as well redo the downstairs bathroom while we're at it. Price tag? If we can repurpose a lot of what we have? At least 30K.

Needless to say, those "last legs" will have to stand up a little longer. My kids now take turns washing the dishes. The fridge still keeps food cold and makes a moderate amount of ice. And my new boots look fabulous!

Grab Bag

There has been much talk in my household about what we could do to help those who have been devastated by the fires. My kids voluntarily cleaned out their closets and gathered toys and clothing items they could donate.

Sifting through their 'discard' pile I was surprised by what had been cast aside. "You love this spy toy/sword/nerf gun/batman thingy," I would say to them. "Mooooommm," they'd retaliate in a manner that all but said, "Be happy we are getting rid of stuff – don't ruin it!"

The idle banter over things became more serious. "What would you grab?" I asked them and their dad, Keith. "If you were granted only a few minutes to throw your most precious items together because you had to evacuate our home, leave your room for good, what would you take?"

My mind immediately went to the obvious – photo albums, important papers. But I was also struck with a sick sense of urgency, as I know that all these items are not in a central location or even appropriately organized. It would be a haphazard grab fest at best. And truly, when I stood outside watching the flames roar toward my house, would those be the items I was glad I had spent my time grabbing up?

Kamden, who is eight, hemmed and hawed. The likeliness of this happening was something he could not fathom and as such, could not think of a single thing. Keith, admittedly, went for the obvious, "The photo albums in the family room." These were albums that were painstakingly put together during our family's early years when I still used film and had it developed. "And my computer," he added. Of course. Losing one's computer these days would be akin to losing an appendage.

They all turned to me. My turn. After pausing to give it some thought, and based on what others are grabbing (or not), I decided I would grab the mess of boxes with 'un-scrap-booked' photos and papers in them – no one has ever really seen those, after all; my computer because it too has new digital photos and writings and precious email correspondences from over the years; my piles of ideas and writings; the writing my kids have done that hang on the walls in our kitchen - their thoughts at those ages could never be replaced. I would also grab my answering machine for it has on it a message from two years ago when Kendall was in the hospital that always lifts me up when I hear it. I would grab the '40 tent' table marker my father recently gave me, a re-gift from twenty-five years ago. There are so many things, I confess, it is hard to narrow it down.

Kendall, who just turned eleven, stated decidedly and without hesitation exactly what he would grab. "My 'micro foam' pillow, a stuffed animal – King, and the picture of our family with the dog." "What about your new Wii game you just bought with your birthday money?" He shrugged his shoulders, shook his head, "No," and continued about his business.

Kamden quickly jumped in, finally deciding what he would grab. "Woofy (his favorite stuffed animal), my blanket and my pillow." What's with the pillows? Comfort, I guess. It fascinates me that they wouldn't take any of their toys or games or anything else they just 'had to have'. Nothing of any real monetary value would have been grabbed by anyone in our family. I will never look at their pillows the same way again.

What would you grab?

Change Your Environment. Change Your Life.

The other day I needed to pick up some work from a colleague's house. Upon arrival, she greeted me at the door looking out of sorts and out of breath. When I asked how she was, she replied, "I don't know. But I am moving furniture around." "I do that all the time," I confessed, "since I was a little girl!" This bit of knowledge allowed her to continue, "It makes me feel better when I'm down." "Me too." I agreed. Then I gave her a Kathleen Melton philosophy, "Change your environment. Change your life." She looked as though she had never connected the two, but I could see the saying resonating for her.

This exchange stayed with me. We all do different things to help move us forward – one thing I do is move furniture around. Often. In fact, I recently felt drained and stuck professionally, so I rearranged my office furniture. This action made me feel better immediately and I realized that the reason the exchange between this colleague and me lingered in my mind was because I witnessed someone else doing what I do in a moment of need - changing an environment to change life.

Here are some ideas on how you can Change Your Environment, Change Your Life.

1. Move your furniture around. Let your furniture float in the middle of the room. Don't get stuck on the idea that a sofa has to be against the wall or a bed has to have two nightstands. I literally

had my bed floating in the middle of my room for a long time because that's where the best view is out my bedroom window. Or skew your furniture, even just one item. Sometimes right angles can be so boring. Put things off center, angle them. Or just move it. Simply move a piece of furniture into another location. I love having the leather storage ottoman (which I had originally bought for the family room) at the foot of my bed. I can always move it back!

2. Add some life. A simple plant or bouquet of flowers can go a long way. Buy whatever you find beautiful at that moment, not one that you think will work in your surroundings. If you loved it at that moment, it will work for you in this moment. I hesitated the other day buying a yellow flowering plant for my entry because nothing in my house coordinates with yellow. But it made me smile and made me happy and that is coordination enough.
3. Remove the clutter. I know this is a big task for some people, but even doing something as small as one area that makes you cringe everyday can go a long way to making you feel more in control of your environment and of your life. Swipe all the junk into a basket and hide it, or throw it out, or give away three things a day from the space (a perfect strategy for a closet), or actually spend the time to sort items/paperwork/junk into keep, discard, and file piles. Whatever you choose, find a way to give your eyes and your psyche a place to rest – an uncluttered place to rest. In the new clear and open space, you will be able to open yourself up to new ideas and thoughts because all the other crap won't be clogging your mind.
4. Delegate. Nothing depresses me more that a filthy house. I am one of the few people I know who actually like to clean, but even I can't keep up with the dirt, laundry and grime in my house on a regular basis. So hire someone to clean your house and to clean up your garden so that when you do have a moment to yourself, you can enjoy your environment – both inside and out – either in a quite moment alone, or with your family.
5. Get rid of old photos. Stop looking at your past and replace (at least some) photos with something you want to do in your future.

6. Give to charity. My mother and my youngest son both hold on to everything. The only way I can get them to part with anything is to make it about someone else. And trust me, there is someone else out there that would benefit from all of the stuff you could part with. Oh, and giving to charity or the needy makes you feel good about yourself (it changes your life for the better).

Ultimately, if all else fails, move. Don't laugh. You would then have to go through all your stuff, give a bunch of it away, toss some of it, move your furniture, and hire someone to help you rearrange it where you wind up. Evidently, it's a good market to buy so check out the offerings. And a new neighborhood is also a new environment.

House "Work"

My house is having a mid-life crisis. It is feeling a bit neglected and way, way, way behind the Joneses. A similar house down our street just got a major renovation. Mine is only asking for a bit of a facelift. Add a little here, remove, resurface and fill in cracks there. Upon initial glance, my house looks good. Dressed in designer furnishings mixed with bargain finds and imbued with a definite sense of style, it more that passes inspection if all you do is a quick walk through. Look a little closer and the age begins to show.

But I can't keep up. Er, I mean my house can't keep up. First of all, I can't afford it right now. Secondly, if I added on, it would be just that much more square footage to clean on a regular basis. Lastly, I like the scuffs, the wear and tear that are visible once you sit and relax in one of the many rooms. My house is lived in. There are no "off limits" areas or rooms that are "saved for good." The marks and gentle damage are all signs of the love and lives that happen here.

Yes, the windows need to be replaced and the dishwasher has all but fallen apart. But tearing down and rebuilding or completely remodeling to keep up with the Joneses is not something I am interested in. I would rather spend my time enjoying my home and all the fun we have in it. This is a gathering spot for friends and family. It is where a lot of other kids want to come and play. And I like it that way. If I (my house) 'had work done,' all that would change. We would not be able to have people over for a long time, as there is always a recovery process involved – who wants a gaggle of boys running riot through a freshly renovated home?

So I choose to live with the imperfections, for they reveal time and character. And one day, when life is a bit quieter and we are alone (and that much older), the house and I may be ready for some nip and tuck work.

A Drip Investment Melody

Drip. Drip. Drip. Drip. Scratch. Scratch. Scratch. Scratch. There are many songs about the rain in California – the most ironic one this time of year being the one that melodically says it never does.

The last bout of rain caused my family room ceiling to leak. Again. Drip. Drip. Drip. And, even worse on the "What's going on with your house scale," the rain forced a rat from the outside to find it's way inside my walls. Scratch. Scratch. Scratch.

Between the dripping and the scratching in the walls I feel like I am in some sort of ancient torture ritual. And in true form, I did what I deemed the only appropriate response – I screamed. Loudly. For a long time. As though it might scare the rat away and block the leak. My kids thought it was hilarious. They started yelling too. And after the ritual was complete, I took action. Who knew that the plans of action for drips and rats would be so similar? Blame it on the rain.

Action 1: Locate it. The drip was easy to locate. Several buckets found their new home directly underneath it. The rat was a bit more difficult, although it seemed stuck in the wall between the den and the garage.

Action 2: Figure out where it's getting in. After my own amateur assessment of the situation, I realized I had to call in the professionals. Nick Lopez, a general contractor, came and cut a hole in my ceiling. Thank god there was no mold (from the rain or anything else). And the thought of the rat finding it's way to this open hole and into my house was horrifying. Stanley Pest Control was called to see if they could figure out where the rat was getting in (and take it away!). As fabulous and helpful as both of these professionals were, I struck out.

Action 3: Expose it. Nick came back and cut another hole in my ceiling in an attempt to locate where the leak is originating. Grates were checked and re-covered around the house to ensure no other rat would get in. Droppings were found in the garage. Ewwww. It was time to move onto the next level.

Action 4: Force it out. Yes, I tried to force my ceiling to leak. Lots of water was run in various places trying to force the drip to happen. There are very few times in life when you want your ceiling to leak, when you wait and pray for the drip, drip, drip. This was one. And of course, when you want something like that to happen, when you wait for it to happen – it doesn't. Just like the rat. Pounding on the walls, setting out bait, trying to force the critter to show itself (again, not something I ever would wish to be a party to), were all in vain. It wouldn't come out. Just like the drip.

Action 5: Wait. This is where you have to realize you can't force Mother Nature. Not a drip or a rat. And yes, when it rained again a few days later, it leaked. And I could see from the exposed inner beams approximately where it was originating from – at least from underneath. And the rat stopped scratching. It was not caught. But the scratching stopped and somehow, from my perspective that is good enough for now. So now all I'm left with is the drip, drip, drip, drip.

Action 5: Deal with it. I am assuming this is where it gets expensive. This drip in the family room could be coming from several places: the deck above; or from the corner construction of the second story; or from the roof where the water could be getting in from inappropriate flashing and running down a crevice through the second story walls and making its way down to the first story ceiling (groan). I'm sure that it will somehow miraculously become obvious before things get torn up any more. Or before the leak gets worse. Or before the next big storm. The peanut butter on the rattraps I can do.

And when all else fails, after doing all that can be done, my go-to action – ignore it. The rat will die in a trap eventually. Or escape. And everyone knows that it never really rains in California so if I can just get through the next few months all will be well and good. The human mind is amazingly adaptable. Drip. Drip-drip. Drip. Drip. Drip-drip-drip-drip-drip. Drip. Do you hear the melody?

All the World is a Stage – And So Is Your Home

Preparing your home for the holidays? Whether you're putting your house up for sale, or would just like your home to look its best for the friends and family that will be dropping in this coming month, Home Staging techniques can make all the difference. Having become increasing popular in the past few years for sellers, Home Staging uses similar guidelines to decorating 'model' homes. The ultimate goal is to make your home appealing and comfortable to others.

There are many professional companies that will come and stage your home for you. But if, like me, you and your family have Guitar Hero 3, new bicycle, and iPhone/iTouch envy, your holiday budget for decorating may be limited. By following a few guidelines, getting your family involved, and using what you have, your home can be transformed into an inviting space that allows you and your guests to focus on what truly matters - family and friends. Let's get started.

1. Clear it. Each year around Thanksgiving, I institute a mandatory "cleaning and clearing" day. Along with our two boys, my husband and I gather up knickknacks, toys, clothing and furnishings no longer wanted or used. Room by room we clear out the clutter, making large piles to donate to local charities. Out of the Closet Thrift store at 18851 Ventura Blvd; the Salvation Army with locations in Van Nuys, Woodland Hills, Granada Hills and Simi Valley; and the Goodwill drop-off center on Ventura Blvd in Tarzana accept large

and small donations. For large furniture donations and clothing, the Vietnam Veterans of America have local pick up services and accept most items in good and/or working condition. You can contact them via their website at www.vva.org.

2. Look In Your Backyard. Once counters, dressers, tables, and mantles are clear and the rooms are empty of any un-necessaries, begin staging them for the holidays. Your garden is an amazing place to begin. Look for beautiful fallen branches to place in a vase, or pinecones to pile on the table. Clear vases can turn anything from your backyard - leaves, flowers, fruits, berries, or branches into a simple and beautiful artistic holiday display. Bringing nature into your home is calming and showcases what your property has to offer.

3. Co-ordinate the Flow. Choosing a few key colors and using them on any surface throughout my house, I establish uniformity from room to room. Throws, pillows, frames, wrapping paper, ribbon, table and bed linens, candles – all these items, if in your chosen colors and strategically placed around your home, will unite and polish your decorating scheme.

4. Food and Fragrance. Oranges, cranberries and cloves placed in various sizes of clear bowels and vases are set on the empty counters and tables throughout my house. A fragrance infuser completes the montage. Alisa Davies from Alexander-Harrison at 18643 Ventura Blvd in Tarzana sells Xela Infusers that come in many subtle scents. Upon opening the 'Christmas Tree' fragrance infuser and arranging the sticks, we both felt the need for eggnog. It made every room in my house smell like a fresh cut Christmas tree, and it should last the entire season.

5. Say it With Words. Decorate with what you love. I love words, so I decorate with them. Framed cards, old advertisements from magazines, inexpensive canvas prints, and literally, just a word on a colorful card artfully placed sends a strong and simple message. I love my small "Be" sculpture by Tamara Hensick, also available at Alexander/Harrison. I change the word out by season and the simplicity strikes a chord with nearly everyone who enters my home.

6. Dress your tables. This time of year, I always have my table set. Even when I am not having a dinner party or expecting company, it always looks as though I am. I recently worked with Nicole Nodelman of Interiors by Nicole to dress up a table for Thanksgiving. Working at a home with no fine table linens, we raided the bed linen cupboard, found sheets in the chosen holiday colors, and Nicole expertly tied up the sides with ribbon. It worked beautifully. To create an instant centerpiece, place a small empty box in the middle of the table and drape it with matching pillowcases. Surround it with cuttings from your backyard, top it with a decoration or frame and you're done!
7. Music. With the scents and visuals taken care of, your final touch is the emotion of music. Chose something that you love, a variety of music and artists that are appropriate to this time of year and set your stereo to 'repeat'. CD Trader at 18926 Ventura Boulevard has a great selection of new and used CD's. My personal favorites are the compilations that showcase a variety of artists.

Finally, once your home is staged, don't forget to fill it with a cast of characters: Family, friends, neighbors and perhaps those few people that you've been wanting to get to know but haven't had the right event to invite them over. Now's the time. No excuses are ever needed to gather during the holidays. See you at home.

Home Life vs. House Envy

House envy. It makes your stomach upset and your mood dark. Have you ever felt it? As an avid open house attendee, there are many beautiful properties on the market that I have seen and really liked. One I even insisted my family see. It was way out of my price range, but still, for whatever reason, I felt this outing was a worthwhile use of our time.

Let me just state that I am by nature not an envious person. I am happy for people that work hard for what they have and I honestly believe that there is enough good to go around for everyone. That being said, I recently walked into a house that was like my house on a massive dose of steroids – it was literally everything I had ever dreamed of having in a home. It was so beautiful, so my style and taste with an amazing yard and view and in such a well maintained, secluded neighborhood that I was immediately envious. It was not a pleasant feeling.

The owners, a lovely young family whom I've known for years, had designed and built this house from their dreams. They were involved in every little detail – right down to the positioning of the outlets horizontally in the baseboards – because this was their opportunity to make their dream come true.

Looking at photographs of the process and listening to the husband and wife talk, it changed from just a house that was built, to a home that was created. It had been designed around the way they would live. It was large, but felt comfortable because of the layout, the way the space flowed, because it was not ostentatious, and because it felt like it had been standing for many, many, years.

The next day, driving my two kids and their friends, I was privy to a conversation that took me off guard - house talk among grade schoolers. One asked my youngest son, "So is your house big? Mine is small, but I have a big yard." And then the barrage of comparisons began: "Have you ever seen so-and-so's house? It's a mansion!" "I had a playdate with a friend whose pool is like a hotel - with a slide!" "He has a huge room with his own bathroom!" And on it went. A house-by-house evaluation amongst eight and eleven year olds. Boys, even!

But what I noticed was that there was no envy in their conversation. Things just were what they were. I wondered why it was different for them. Perhaps because all they focused on was the size of the structure or pool rather than what went on inside the house? Perhaps because all the possibilities of life lay in front of them? Would that mean that I then had felt envy because my possibilities are becoming less? This thought was so depressing. I immediately shunned it, realizing how ridiculous it was. Life can change day to day. And my possibilities are endless (damn it!).

My house envy faded, but that particular property will always be on my list of favorites. Right below my own home, where my family has built our own memories, created a big beautiful life and designed our happiness. And that is strong foundation for a dream house.

A Sign of the Times

Five offers. Two escrows. Three back up offers. All have fallen through in the past six months. Is it a sign of the times or a sign of owners and realtors not knowing how to play by the rules of the housing market today? "The first offer was sight unseen. We should have known they would back out," owner Shari (last name with held) told me in describing the events surrounding her property in Tarzana.

"The back up offer we had fell through as well. Then, the second time we were in escrow, we gave the buyer an extension - at their request. Two days after his loan came through, the buyer decided he couldn't make the payments and backed out. We never should have given him an extension without contingencies."

My kids think that Shari's house is the coolest house they have ever seen - because of the "secret rooms," or "nooks and crannies" as they describe it. They think it's an easy sell, "It's the kind of house I want to buy when I grow up," Kendall states matter-of-factly. I smile. For him it's not that it is a great family house in a nice neighborhood with fantastic schools, or that it has a big grassy play area, lap pool with diving board, basketball area, an open floor plan, a big master with walk in closet and a loft, four other bedrooms and three and a half baths -- it is all about the cool "secret rooms."

The "secret room" – or bonus suite in real estate terms, which is truly a self-sufficient guest unit complete with bathroom, closet and wood burning fireplace - is actually, and I am not exaggerating, accessed by turning a hidden knob in the built-in bookshelves in the family room. One entire panel of the bookshelf swings open to reveal a narrow staircase that leads up to the "secret room." "It's soooo super cool!" my kids exclaim. I have to agree. It's definitely the room I would want to claim as my own if I bought this house.

So why isn't this house selling? Are the potential buyers bringing their kids over to see the house as well? Are they getting in touch with their own inner child? If they were, there would be a lot of fighting for this house to be theirs. "People seem to be looking for excuses not to buy," observes Shari's husband Greg, who has been fielding the offers and handling the escrows. "But this is truly a great property for an amazing price, right now."

"Before we listed our house we got several offers," Shari tells me. "But they were much lower than our asking price so we turned them down." In hindsight, they would do things very differently. But how could they have known? They took buyers at their word. They put their trust in others to do the right thing in a business arrangement, to their own detriment. And, ultimately, they could not have predicted the change in the market.

Statistically, there are still many areas doing well. Holding strong. Perhaps people are reading the headlines and feeling tentative. Who knows. Shari and Greg bought another house before they listed theirs. It did not occur to them that they would have any problem selling. And they did not want to sell without having found another house they loved. So, whether due to the market or just their individual circumstance, they are now motivated to sell their house.

"You take a chance either way," Shari confides. "Whether you buy first or sell first, each has it's own set of risks." And each individual or family has their own risk tolerance.

"We are actually in escrow again. We hope this one works out," Shari says confidently. When I look at the history of their experience, I note that the house has been on the market for less than six months, which in their price range – even though the asking price has changed in that time - is evidently not unusual.

I am also quick to point out that they have had many offers, many escrows, and many backup offers. The house is obviously desirable and people continue to make offers (much to my kids chagrin, it is not them). It has not sat stagnant at all. And that is a good sign. In any market. Of course, the best sign is the one in front of the house that states, "Sold".

A Backyard's Journey

When we bought our home eight and a half years ago the backyard was a major selling point. It was lush, with a flat area, a pool, a waterfall koi pond, and hill that provided privacy. Shortly after moving in, however, it became the bane of my existence. The animals that evidently inhabited my hillside ate the koi, - after my then two year old had named each one - leaving blood all over the concrete. The large possums and raccoons would come right up to my back door and scratch furiously. The grass died because the backyard was too shady from all the overgrown foliage, and worst of all, I was afraid to sit outside on our beautiful porch after dark because of all the frightening noises emanating from the hill. One day, a blue herring landed and finished off the last of the koi, a swarm of ducks landed in the pool, and that night, I found a rat floating on the pool cover. That was the last straw. I was ready to move. I felt like I was living in a botched episode of Wild Kingdom.

After a few months the drama subsided until the neighbors above us requested to trim our thirty years old pine trees to improve their view. They said they had done it regularly with the previous owners, insisted on paying for it all, won over my son (and thus me) with sweetness and seemed so nice and grandparently that I agreed. Big Mistake. The crew they hired butchered five of our giant trees. Logs were dropped into our pool, damaging the plaster and surrounding concrete. Within a month the trees were dead from a pine beetle attack. My neighbor was nonplussed.

He said it was not his responsibility. The nice man that he had appeared to be in the beginning had vanished – along with my trees.

Thus began the adventure with (and probable reason for neglect of) our backyard. We hired a company to come in a remove the dead trees along with a few others and to clear a bit of the hill so that the critters living amongst the overgrown bushes and ivy would have to find another overgrown backyard inhabit.

Eight years, two growing boys, a dog, and a broken sprinkler system later, our backyard is nearly desolate. It bears no semblance to the backyard of the house we bought. It has finally reached a point where doing something is not just an option – it is mandatory. But if I was going to spend money on the house, truthfully, it was in desperate need of new windows and a paint job. Did it desperately need grass? Not really. But then I had my second son's eight-year-old birthday party to plan. He did not want it at Ultra zone, Chuck E. Cheese or any other play place – much to my chagrin. He wanted all his friends to come over to our house so that they could all play on the hill. The hill has, in the last few months become the 'boy' place to play. And after an evening watching ten boys climb and play and use their imaginations for over four hours on our hill, my husband and I decided that is where our house improvement budget would go – into creating a backyard that the kids would want to hang out in with their friends. "We only have ten years left before they both leave the house," I told Keith. I want our house to be where all the kids want to hang out. Let's put the money in the backyard. He agreed.

I tore idea sheets out of magazines, researched plants and shrubs and Keith and I drew up what we thought would be the ultimate backyard. Sports court, grassy area, fortress with access on and off the hill, paths on the hill, plants to hold the hill that are sturdy enough to trample, and a fire pit to roast marshmallows and hotdogs and cozy up at night.

We would have to push back part of the hill to make the sports court big enough. Nothing overly fancy, just a place to shoot hoops and to play a good game of handball. I could not figure out where on the hill to build a fortress so I settled on buying a prefabricated one from Yardscape Outdoor Center in Woodland Hills that I would work into my plan. I would put it behind the pool area so the kids could use it when they used the pool – and the pool gate was down – and it would have a ramp onto the hill as well.

I began calling landscapers. Everyone from the neighbor's gardener to landscape architects. The ideas, the explanations of city codes, what could and couldn't be done, and the price ranges were all over the board. I finally decided on John D'Urso of D'Urso landscaping. I had actually consulted him eight years ago during the tree debacle about what I would do once the trees were gone and while I decided not to do anything way back then, I had liked his ideas and demeanor, so I located his number all these years later and called him up. He remembered us as well, and as before, he offered good ideas, was very knowledgeable on appropriate codes and had reasonable rates to achieve our goals.

So now we are in the final planning stages. We haven't quite figured out exactly what we are doing in certain areas (like where to put the fortress), but in others we have. A backyard is a living, breathing entity after all, or at least ours will be once again, once we breathe new life into it. I look forward to sharing this journey with you.

Head to Head: My Backyard Journey Part 2

During our initial walk through of what we planned for our backyard makeover, John D'Urso, our landscape designer said three words that have continued to pop into my mind throughout this process, "Head to head." He was talking about sprinkler coverage – that you need head to head coverage from sprinkler to sprinkler to ensure the survival of new grass (I have never been able to get grass to live in my backyard). But we have not yet laid new grass, still the "head to head" seems to have become a common theme of many issues that have arisen during this project.

Head to Head #1: My Spouse. Without question, there needs to be one person in charge of a project. For this project, that person has been me, or so I thought. I came home one day to find out my husband, Keith, had an entire conversation with John about rounded edges. Keith was under the erroneous impression that he and I had agreed to rounded edges. What the edges were for doesn't even really matter, the fact is, my experience of the conversation was that there were to be no rounded edges, and Keith thought the opposite. Unfortunately, he was the one that was home when John showed up to ask about this. Thankfully, I caught it in time, for the backyard design did not include rounded edges. And where should the end of the fence be? What color finish for the walls? Where will the grass end and other planting begin? How to configure the play structure for the kids? Should there be another step up to the sports court? Where and how to retrain the dog to do her business? Each of these conversations seems to end up in a bit of "head to head" match over what one person thought we had already decided. It's all worked out so far because ultimately Keith and I see eye to eye (after going head to head) on most issues.

Head to Head #2: My Neighbors. It's amazing how a dumpster and a port-a-potty bring out the neighbors. I have not had this many conversations with my neighbors in years. Evidently, there were even conversations taking place in front of my house about my project when I wasn't home. Property lines are a big issue. Fences are another. Planting that may affect another's landscaping (or future landscaping plans) is another. I had no idea bamboo was a bad idea, thank you, John. Ultimately, my neighbors are all well meaning and reasonable people and while we may not agree on the issues, we did resolve them amicably. And I do hope we continue to speak this much when the project is done.

Head to Head #3: Children and Dogs. A backyard all torn up and full of equipment and trash is a recipe for disaster for kids and dogs. As such, my boys have had to reluctantly play inside the house or in the front yard. They have had to use their imaginations to figure out what to do with themselves without a backyard. They've also had to clean up dog poop in all kinds of new places – our dog now goes where she can – by the pool, on the hill, under the tree, on walks. Thankfully, my youngest, Kamden, doesn't mind picking up the poop on walks. And my oldest, Kendall, has found a new fondness for walking the dog up and down our street. We have all developed a new appreciation for our front porch, but we all look forward to my being able to tell them, "Go out back and play!"

Head to Head #4: My landscaper and his crew. This is, oddly, where the least "head to head" issues have occurred. Other than a few clarifications, the crew that has been working on my house has been amazing. Headed by a very capable man named Jose, these guys are unbelievably talented and professional. They show up every day at 7:30 am. I can actually count on them to be there. How refreshing! John comes and regularly checks on the job and any issues that we have had have been addressed immediately. There have been compromises on both sides, but again, John and his crew know what they are doing and have led us in the appropriate direction.

Head to Head #5: My Property Budget. No matter what I want for my backyard or for my kids, I eventually must come to terms with and work within the confines that my property has to offer. Or more specifically, what my budget for my property can offer me – and how I can make the most of it with numbers 1 through 4 above.

So now I wait patiently for them to finish the hardscape so we can move on to the sprinkler issue. For that is going to be of the utmost importance for me. I want grass to live! I don't want to be walking on dirt anymore. I don't want the kids and dog to track mud and dirt into the house anymore. I want to be able to lie in the grass and look up at the sky with my kids. I am ready to go "head to head" and resolve this issue too. Bring it on.

Tipping Point: My Backyard Journey Part 3

It was very naive of me to think it wouldn't happen. But nearly four weeks into the project, I reached my tipping point. The anxiety attack took me by surprise. Perhaps because in my mind, the project would have been completed by now, and yet I was still facing at least another week and a half of work. Or perhaps because I am looking at my trashed backyard, the dirt and grime that renders everything useless to me and the boys, but somehow makes it way into the house everyday - forcing all of us to keep up with the extra cleaning. Or perhaps it was the sums of money on my most recent bank statement showing as "cashed" from my checking account for three consecutive weeks to pay for this (with two to go) - and wondering if it was worth it. Keith, my husband, said that I am just second guessing myself. That our backyard and the choices we made for it are going to be fabulous. I calmed down a bit and finally got a hold of myself. Ironically, that is when things went from not so bad to worse.

After a difficult and very unpopular decision I made to have the stucco a dark green, the color that was put on my new walls was a light bluish grey. I chose a La Habra color from their color chart. Evidently, they did not have it in stock, so John, my landscaper, went to El Dorado and chose what they recommended would be the closest to my original choice. Then it was mixed and put on. Without consulting me. The most humorous part of this was that John and I went back and forth for two days on the color choice. Again, my choice was not popular as John readily admits he errs on the side of safe and boring, but ultimately, I knew the dark green would look great in our overall design. And it most likely would have if the color had come out correctly. Would you put Behr brand green paint on your walls after the color that was chosen was Benjamin Moore brand green? Probably not, not without approval, because there is no way these two colors from two different companies would be the same. Doesn't it seem reasonable to apply that logic to other color applications that are being hemmed and hawed over? So now the walls have to be "fog coated". Whatever that means. And if that doesn't work, we may have to just paint it green. There goes my desire for 'maintenance free.'

The next day, no one was in our backyard. For the first time in nearly four weeks, our backyard was void of activity. When John showed up the following day to inspect the color mishap – no need to come right away, as evidently stucco needs time to cure and lighten up ("I hope not," I said, "it's already too light), there was still no one in our backyard. "I miss Jose and the guys," I stated glibly to John, wondering why he hadn't called to tell me or give me an explanation. Picking up on my not so subtle, but polite, topic, he explained that an irate wife of a client was making all kinds of changes to their job, screaming at his guys inappropriately, being overly demanding and turning a one day job into a four day job. "Ah, so if I was an irate client, I'd have the guys here?" John laughed at this and apologized for having to pull the guys off my job, but evidently, the husband of this irate woman has been a wonderful client of John's over the years. Now, if that had just been explained to me in the beginning, I would understand. I am a reasonable person, who in fact, had just that day also been yelled at inappropriately by an irate client. I can only suppose my client, like John's client, was having a bad day and took it out on me because he felt he had the right to – perhaps because no one ever calls him on his atrocious behavior. So I guess if you deal with enough people who think they have the right to yell at you and treat you poorly simply because you are doing some work for them or with them, well then, I understand not wanting to bring up any issue unless you have to. One day John and I, and hopefully you, will shock clients when we finally choose appropriate behavior instead of their business. But I digress.

So because my backyard work was put on hold for someone else and because the walls will now have to be modified somehow, I had to change the install date of the fortress – I didn't want to risk getting paint on it and the ground still has to be prepped for sod before the fortress can go in. Sadly, I am still trying to figure out a date that will work for both that company, for me and for the work that still needs to be done.

On this same day, I had to have a plumber come to my house because of an odor issue that I suspected might be water leaking under my house. Completely unrelated to the landscaping - thank God, but that was my first thought. Turns out it was my sewage pipes, kitchen pipes and washing machine pipes that were cracked, leaking, old and ultimately in need of replacement under my house. Michael McKeough from Super Plumbing, Inc., was a plumber I had not used before and the only one that we could get anyone to recommend after many, many, many phone calls. He spent, and I kid you not, nine full hours under my house cutting, testing, clearing and fixing pipes and connections that had been doing the job since the house was built in 1961. He would come out of the crawl space only for more parts, looking like a mad scientist. He was very thorough and spelled out my options concisely. I chose to have all the problems fixed while I had his full attention, so he politely cancelled his other appointments to deal with my serious plumbing emergency – which continued for another three hours the following day. I was gracious and thankful – never irate or demanding, even as the clocked ticked away and I saw all my beautiful new plants slowly disappearing down the drain – figuratively and literally. After that plumbing bill there would not be any cash left over for the beautiful plants I had chosen and budgeted for to complete my backyard....

So now with clean new pipes, I wander my backyard. Anxiety gone. Tipping Point nearly passed. John has assured me that the wall will be taken care of, and I know it will as he is very professional and we have a good working relationship. The kids, the dog, Keith and I all hung out by the pool (after some hosing down) and actually used our backyard space as a family for the first time in a month. Doing so allowed us to see a few things we would change when the guys returned to work in our backyard. Minor things – where not to put a sprinkler head because we'd rather extend the existing stone there, where the grass line should end and eventual (sigh) planting would one day begin. These changes would not have happened if circumstances hadn't forced a tipping point for me to get through and granted a reprieve from the work, which allowed us to rediscover our yard before the final stage – before it was too late. I do believe that things happen for a reason and that what goes around comes around and how you choose to handle situations and people affects many other aspects of your life – including your backyard. Our yard will actually be better due to this tipping point and because of how we handled it. I am, however, looking forward to seeing Jose in my backyard again on Monday morning...

Ramp It Up

My off ramp is disgusting. To clarify, the exit off the freeway that I take to get to my house is dreadful. I recently had the luxury of going to San Diego for a weekend alone. Just me. No kids. No responsibility, just time to reflect and rejuvenate. It was wonderful. And by Sunday evening I was truly relaxed, recharged and ready to see my family again.

Approaching my off ramp I turned my blinker on and I felt like I was home. Then, I cringed. Because I was driving down my off ramp, and was reminded of every nagging thing that needed to be done. Of the endless to-do lists and never finished projects. Of reality. The tension immediately crept back into my neck. And yes, all this was due to the visual wreckage that is my off-ramp.

Seriously, this small stretch of freeway exit is so embarrassing that when someone visits my house for the first time, I've been known to send them directions to my house via the off-ramp before mine or after mine, regardless of whether they are coming from the north or the south (actually east or west but that is another article about the 101). Both off ramps are equally offensive. From either direction, I cringe at the unpleasantness presented to me and all those who use it.

"Doesn't she have anything better to think about," you may be asking yourself. Well, yes, I have lots of things to think about, but usually at the end of the day, or if I am going home, I want to relax and unwind and not think about anything. But I can't 'not think' about the trash, the graffiti, the weeds, the litter, or the homeless beggars that I encounter day in and day out and that for some reason, all of us who live near this off-ramp, tolerate. It is, after all, the first introduction to our neighborhood, to our homes.

I am relieved to report that I am not alone. One of the many people I spoke with nailed it on the head.

"Exiting our off-ramp is like being dumped into a ghetto," describes Steve Webber who has lived at this exit with his wife Nancy since 1970.

Yes, I know, a 'ghetto' with an average house price in the 'points', but it is not the neighborhood we are describing or discussing here. It is the immediate feelings one gets from the off ramp experience. Don't lose focus.

"The functionality is inappropriate and it looks bad," Steve continues, validating that I am not crazy. "Often times we bypass it and exit at the ramps before ours or after ours."

Tifani Kunze, another resident who has lived at this exit most of her life reiterates. "I don't understand why the surrounding off ramps are so much nicer. It has to be the same people." Indeed, it is. After calling Councilman Dennis Zine's office, I learned that off ramps are supposedly a county function handled by CalTrans. I will note that some attempt was made to brick and concrete part of it over, similar to what was done on surrounding off-ramps, but the work wasn't completed. Landscaping was not done. Either that or it wasn't executed properly.

Searching the CalTrans website, I could barely navigate through all the text and mission statements, much less find a way to contact someone regarding my particular off ramp. So I realize this will be a lengthy and uphill battle. But I've no plans to move and would like to change it so I can enjoy my time here even more. So what can I do about it? I can tell you about it. We can talk about it and find other like-minded people to form a group and take action.

If your off-ramp makes you cringe, email me and let me know where it is and what you are willing to do about it. Conversely, if you are lucky enough to live near of one of the many lovely off ramps, please email me pictures for continued inspiration. See you at home – via the round about way from any off ramp other than my own.

Repurpose the Rooms that Taunt You

Which part of your house do you not use? How much money have you spent money furnishing it in the hopes that you would use it? Does it sometimes seem to taunt you? My formal dining room taunted me. It was used maybe three times in eight years, and then only as a buffet room, not as the fabulous, sit-and-talk-for-hours-with-friends room I had imagined.

I couldn't take the taunting anymore. So I emptied it out. Removed every bit of furniture and lighting and stood there in my new empty space feeling free. Who said this had to be a dining room? It has a pocket door, a window with shutters and an opening to the living room. Hmmm, if I were able to close the opening off with curtains, this room would be able to be completely blacked out. This could be the perfect space for a screening room. After all, the kids have over taken the TiVo in the family room (our only TV) and my shows are constantly being 'accidentally' deleted to make room for theirs.

So I graphed the room out on paper. Took precise measurements and began the hunt. It is a bit of an odd sized room (it is a dining room after all) so I would have to find a sofa that fit perfectly....and that would take time. I also would have to find a TV that I would want to look at, or a way to hide it, and a console that would blend with the style of the living room, as this room opens to the living room. The curtains would be easy. Swing arm rods with curtains like those already hanging in the living room to tie the two rooms together.

Deep, dark chocolate brown paint on one wall was the perfect backdrop for a plasma screen. I consulted with an expert about the height and distance the TV should be from the sitting area based on screen size. Once armed with all the necessary information, items began to fall into place. I found the sofa that fit exactly at Z Gallerie in the Promenade Woodland Hills. I ordered a console from KB Contractors in Canoga Park. Swing arm curtain rods from Restoration Hardware catalog. Lighting from Ballard Designs catalog. And finally, the television and surround sound from Costco. We added our own accents of old movie projectors, cameras and books on cinema and film just for contrast to the new technology.

This previous dead space in my house is now used everyday. It is a cozy, comfy space, where my kids like to read. Where I sometimes escape in the middle of the day for a bit of quiet. Where my husband and I congregate at night to marvel at how amazing "Heroes," and "24" look in HD – it's like watching an altogether different program.

But mostly, the room no longer taunts me. It is now used daily. I gave up convention and made it my own, my family's own, into a space that serves us and our needs. For it is our house and every room should be useful to us as we live our lives now, regardless of its original intent. And it has quickly become a favorite room in my house.

Which room would you like to repurpose?

Acknowledgements

Thanking all the people in all the situations who have inspired me would be a book in and of itself. Please know that I am grateful for every moment.

My kids, Kendall and Kamden, you inspire me and teach me everyday. Keith, thank you for supporting my dreams and believing in me.

Harold Medina, thank you for your unending encouragement and for providing me with an outlet for my writing.

Ellen, Forrest, Amy, Kelsie, Kinsey, Kolby, Steve, Ben, Ricki, John, Alberta, Jessica, Alisa, Janeen, and my very first accountability partner, Julie - without you all, I'd have no place to let down my guard.

To all the parents, children and individuals that I encounter on my life's journey, without you, this book and my ongoing articles would not be possible.

And to God for blessing me with this life. I try to find the gratitude moment by moment and to seek out the gift in each situation. Everyday above ground is a blessed day!

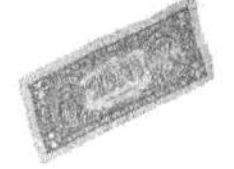

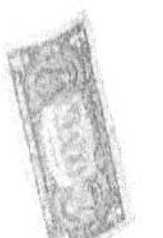

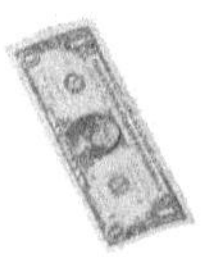

About The Author

Kathleen Melton's third grade teacher, Mr. Collier, had the children in his class write weekly stories, read them aloud to the class, then vote on their favorite story of the week. Kathleen's were often voted the class favorite and her writing career was born. Thank you Mr. Collier.

After graduating from UCLA with a degree in Communications, she went to work as an advertising manager for Showscan Entertainment where she supervised the art direction and writing of the company's advertising campaigns. She left Showscan for a Director of Marketing job at HDLA – High Definition Los Angeles, a specialized post-production facility. From HDLA she moved on to Infinity Filmworks as Director of Creative Development and Business Management. She eventually married her partner, Keith Melton, and they now have two inspirational boys, Kendall and Kamden.

Wanting to return to her first love, Kathleen started writing for the *Los Angeles Daily News* and for various clients. Her two columns, *Home Stretch*™ and her blog, *Tarzana Housewife Trials and Triumphs*™ have become widely read and respected, and garner much feedback. Scraps is a compilation of articles she has written, some published in local newspapers, others not. She is currently exploring the syndication of both columns and working on her next book. To be kept up to date, visit www.KathleenMelton.com.

In between shuttling her kids to sporting activities and writing and working, she makes time to exercise, read and just be.

Enjoy life's little scraps.

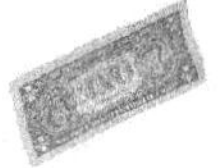

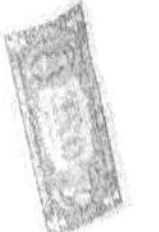